Crash and Learn

Lessons in Business
Featuring 10 Inspiring Business Leaders

Avanti Wisdom Series

Prominence Publishing, www.prominencepublishing.com

ISBN: 978-1-988925-56-1

Contents

Introduction

The inspiration for this book stemmed from my frustration with the pretty pictures that everyone paints about their entrepreneurial journey. If you look at magazine covers and social media posts, it would appear that everyone is killing it! One could assume that all entrepreneurs have perfect lives with the perfect house, car, family and more... except, maybe, you?

Well, don't stress about it because what I know to be true is this—behind every glossy, picture-perfect curtain, there is a crash and burn story to be told. I know this because during the hundreds of podcast interviews I have done, I always ask business owners and entrepreneurs to tell me their "crash and burn story." Inevitably, the guest will answer, "OK, which one?!"

What I have learned from their answers is that a true entrepreneur never crashes and burns... they crash and learn!

They take the miserable experience of failing and turn it into part of their education. It makes them stronger and wiser. And builds their endurance muscle.

A hurricane makes a tree's roots stronger—while it appears the hurricane might uproot the tree, the tree holds on and as a result, becomes even stronger.

And so will you.

I have gathered some of my favorite entrepreneurs and asked them to share their "crash and learn" story. I am honored and applaud them for sharing their experiences. Not everyone wants to put a spotlight on their down times, but by doing so, my co-authors are able to help others.

And that, my friends, is what it is all about.

I hope you enjoy the lessons in these stories as much as I have. I am confident that they will keep you moving forward on your entrepreneurial journey. Embrace the highs and lows, because they all offer incredible experiences and lessons.

Be sure to continue the journey during the down times. It can be tough and a test of will and faith, but I know you can make it through to thrive again. And your experience will be a lesson to others.

Winston Churchill says it best: "If you're going through hell, keep going."

Yes, you will get to the other side.

Move Forward,

David Mammano

Founder, Avanti Entrepreneur Network

CHAPTER 1

Trust the Journey

By David Mammano

As a serial entrepreneur (I've launched 10+ businesses and brands), I can assure you I have made my fair share of mistakes. In fact, looking back, I think I've spent more time crashing than succeeding, yet, I am still here! Perhaps my luck has remained just a touch ahead of my mistakes.

One thing I have learned for sure is that "failing forward" is an important part of the process. Just as a hurricane actually strengthens the roots of a tree, adversity strengthens the resolve of an entrepreneur. We learn, we grow and then we move forward.

I launched my first business in 1995. It was a magazine called *Next Step Magazine* and we helped high school students with planning for college, career, and life. Print media was still a viable option back then so we thrived. I started out with a local edition in my hometown of Rochester, New York, and we soon franchised the concept with editions in every state.

Next Step Magazine (later changed to *NextStepU*) was a hit! We had distribution in more than 20,000 high schools and became a multi-million dollar business. The company was on the *Inc. Magazine* 5000 List three times in a row; locally, we were a Top 100 growth company. We won some national content awards, I was nominated for small business of the year, an ethics award, and more.

Wow! It was a fun time and I was amazing! Everything I touched turned to gold. I felt like I was born for massive entrepreneurial success! Of course, I'm being facetious and grandiose here but I did feel that way sometimes. The reality was very far from the truth: the day of reckoning came.

That darn digital revolution was slowly creeping forward over the past few years and soon started to take hold. Print was quickly becoming an outdated technology with teens and advertisers were noticing.

Our client renewal calls—which formerly were pleasant— turned into conversations about how they still loved *NextStepU*, but they wanted to get away from print. They would continue asking us about our digital options which were a fraction of the cost for them. Our clients' budgets were being slashed, a result of the Great Recession of 2008-2009 happening at the time.

Our team feverishly worked to create and sell the value of combined packages that included print and digital as pieces of the same pie. We created "bundled packages" and sold the case for print as a branding solution.

Our valiant efforts worked for a while but eventually, selling print advertising became as exciting as selling a horse and buggy after Henry Ford launched the Model T automobile. Eventually, we succumbed to the pressure. We retired the printed magazine and went all online. It broke my heart. I was a print guy! As a kid, I delivered the afternoon newspaper to my neighborhood. Then in college, I become the advertising manager for the campus newspaper. Then, of course, I started my own magazine.

"Damn this digital revolution!" I would often say.

But here we were, deep in Phase One of the digital revolution and I had to either sink or swim. As it turns out, I did both.

As we transitioned the company, I was determined to keep my entire team. They were hard-working, dedicated superstars, many of whom helped me build the company from the beginning stages. This is when I started to dig my hole.

I became an even more frenetic entrepreneur. Instead of re-focusing our business model into one focused mission, I started three new products under the company umbrella. I was also trying to keep *NextStepU* alive online.

The first new idea was a college planning retail center called "NextStepU College Planning Center." I saw the success of Sylvan Learning and Huntington Learning Centers so I took their model and focused it on college planning. We would help students access their innate skills and then match those students to the right college, college majors and ultimately, careers. I told people, "We're like a guidance counselor on steroids."

NextStepU College Planning Center was a very expensive model. There was high rent, payments to the counselors doing the work and then the marketing. At the end of the day, the profit margin was very little and not many people bought our core product even though the research showed they would. Never trust research! (More on that later.) My manic, entrepreneurial nature had not taken the time to fully plan out this model, and after two years, I closed the center.

The second new product was another printed product called *LINK Magazine*. Our target was high school guidance counselors and the goal was helping them assist their students' college and career planning. We figured the counselors were an older demographic that still read print and we were right! The magazine was a hit and the school counselors enjoyed it. We provided the magazine for free, selling college advertising to support it. It's what we did for *NextStepU* Magazine back in the day.

About 18 months later, one of my former franchisees made me an offer to purchase *LINK Magazine*. Since I was cash-strapped and needed the money, I took his offer and sold it to him.

The third product was one for which I was massively excited. Our research with high schools and students indicated an overwhelmingly positive response so we moved ahead. We were starting an online school! We called it "Next Step Academy" and its mission was teaching life skills to high school students. The courses focused on aspects such as: dressing for success, speaking in public, interviewing skills and social media etiquette. The product was given to high schools for free and they had the freedom of choosing how best to use it for their students. Then we had college recruitment advertising pay for it.

We built the site, got some high schools to sign up and colleges to sponsor. But then, a lot of... crickets. The Common Core Curriculum was instituted that year so schools had a tough time adding anything new to their curriculums. While we did get some colleges to sponsor the program, high schools were just not implementing the service!

This is a good segue to quickly discuss research. Be careful when researching for a new company or product. The people you use for your dataset will often tell you what you want to hear. Your idea probably does sound great to them and ideally, they would use the new service. They don't want to hurt your feelings so they will tell you all the good things. However, it doesn't matter what they tell you, it's their actions that matter.

In my opinion, the best research is an actual sale. When push comes to shove, will the customer actually buy the product? There are ways to test this without building your full-fledged product upfront. For more on this strategy, I suggest reading *The Lean Startup* by Eric Ries. This book is a great resource on how to take the necessary steps to test your product's marketability before going into full product launch mode.

Back to Next Step Academy. After we saw that the high schools were not implementing it, I ended up selling the company to a partner who took the platform in a different direction.

Now, through all of this, I still had the remnants of *NextStepU Magazine*. We had moved everything online, turning it into a content site where the revenue model was a college matching tool. Students entered criteria for what they desired in a college and then receive matches from our list of sponsoring colleges. If a college on their list was of interest, the student could click on the college to request more information. Our college clients were essentially paying us for leads.

NextStepU became a very transactional business and I lost interest quickly. I am not a transactional guy. I like to build relationships through good content and truly help people on their journeys. I ended up selling the website to a person I felt could take it to the next level.

Along my frenetic journey, you may have noticed my manic efforts to save the company I and my great team built through 18 years of blood, sweat and tears. I not only tried to pivot the printed magazine to online, I launched a retail center, a new printed magazine for high school guidance counselors and an online life skills school for teens.

Looking back, whoa! What was I thinking? What a tailspin, what a flurry of attempts to reinvent. At the time, it made sense but now all I see is a manic entrepreneur desperately trying to stay alive. My ego was caught up in the attempt to save some semblance of the initial magazine model. My emotions were tied up in saving my employees and I had a personal mission to keep them because many had helped me build the company from the beginning.

Eventually, I was left with two of my core, die-hard team members and we were grasping at anything to survive. It was at this time that—in my opinion—God stepped in and gave me a lifeline. *You are exactly where you are supposed to be.*

I was in my car when I received a phone call from a guy named Ben. We had met about five years earlier. Ben was calling out of the blue to thank me for the advice I had given him about starting a business. When we met five years before, he was just out of college and wanting to start a business. I always met with people to discuss their ideas because other mentors had done so for me when I was starting out.

On the present call, Ben mentioned that I had given him some ideas at our meeting that helped shape his success and he was reaching out to show his gratitude. I was very touched by this, thanked him for the call and for actually listening to my advice! Before Ben hung up, he said, "You should do this for a living."

I said, "Do what for a living?"

Ben continued, "Help people start or grow businesses."

Bam! His words hit me between the eyes! I thought, "Yes! I could take my highs and lows as an entrepreneur and help people by sharing my experiences."

And that, folks, was the start of David Mammano 2.0 and the Avanti Entrepreneur Network.

The initial idea was a coaching business. This led to events, a podcast, peer groups, a monthly speaker series, annual summits and more. What it has really done is give me a new passion for creating businesses. Today, Avanti is thriving, helping thousands of entrepreneurs by creating original and curated content, events and many other impactful services and experiences.

Although my experience to this point was a crazy—sometimes enjoyable and sometimes petrifying—rollercoaster ride, I wouldn't change a thing. The highs and lows helped shape me and inform how I can help people. Looking back, I am glad I stayed on the rollercoaster. Sometimes, you just have to trust the journey.

I hope my business experiences and my reflections on them have helped you. I wouldn't trade my journey for the world. Even though it was very stressful at times, it helped shape who I am today and how I help people. I have specifically used my roller-coaster ride to create a business model that helps entrepreneurs navigate their decisions. I love it and it's my destiny.

Feel free to use the lessons from my journey to brings success to yours. I am here for you; feel free to contact me through:

AvantiEntrepreneur.com and David@DavidMammano.com.

I pray that you become as awesome as your destiny!

What I Have Learned

I certainly feel like I needed the journey God gave me to get me where I am today. My roots, endurance and resolve are certainly all strengthened. But if I take my experiences to help others move forward faster and with less turbulence, I would suggest the following:

1. **Remove the Emotion.** I was very emotional about both my print magazine business model and my team. Looking back, the writing on the wall was obvious: print was dying and digital was taking over so I should have acted

more quickly. If I had been completely unemotional about the decision, I should have taken stock of the team, their talents and immediately pruned the rose bush, only keeping a few of the members who had digital marketing talents.

2. **What Can You Do with What You Have?** Instead of inventing brand-new products that require new customer bases, I should have considered how to serve our current clients' digital needs. With my core team—after the pruning—we could have created digital marketing solutions that also didn't cost us much or add turbulence to our company. The pivot would have been relatively seamless, since it wasn't too far from our advertising-based model. At the end of the day, we would still get prospective leads for our clients, it was just a different way to skin the cat.

3. **Walk Before Leaping.** This is concept is very counterintuitive for me. I'm often described as "the guy who sees the cliff and just goes for the jump." I'm a living embodiment of the proverbial "build the airplane on the way down." That said, I've learned that there is some wisdom in looking over the cliff before you jump.

As mentioned earlier, the best research you can do is testing the waters with sales. Will people actually commit money to your product, even before you build it? Is there a version you can do without investing a ton of money into it? Don't get hung up on presenting a product that's unfinished. You can always refund the money if you decide not to move forward.

Again, read the book, *The Lean Startup* and google their videos. I wish I did this before frenetically launching products and companies to "save the day."

4. **Revert to Start-Up Mentality.** When you are getting back on your feet with a new product or company, it's easy to forget what it was like when you started the first one. When I started my first company, I didn't take a salary for a few years and worked nights as a waiter. It took a good 3-4 years to get the flywheel turning.

Remember that starting something new is not like turning on a light switch. It takes time, patience and incredible endurance. Now, you certainly may have momentum from your current business because of existing customers, you may have a good reputation in the marketplace and some cash-flow. However, it will take time for the rubber to hit the road on a new—or pivoted— concept. Take a deep breath; in many ways you'll have to act like a start-up all over again.

5. **Planning All Over Again.** My first business was very detailed. I did projected expenses, revenue data, competitor research and much more. These steps did not happen when launching my new business. I was in survival mode and didn't take the time for deep planning. I just figured that we would find a way to make it work. Bad idea.

6. **Gather a Team.** My advice is to get a team together and surround yourself with "A" players that complement your strengths and weakness. Go offsite and hold a retreat. You'll want to really test some concepts with your team and do some deep, financial projections. Make sure to develop a strong sales and marketing strategy. In today's competitive marketplace, you can no longer "build it and they will come." You need to have very purposeful and instigative sales/marketing plans, both inbound and outbound.

About the Author
David Mammano

For more than 20 years, David Mammano has been a serial entrepreneur. Having started seven businesses from scratch, he thrives on starting and growing businesses.

Today he thrives on helping others start or grow their businesses by infusing the latest entrepreneurial principles into their strategy.

Relevant experiences include being a three-time *Inc. Magazine* 5000 Growth Company, the host of *The Avanti Entrepreneur* podcast, a TEDx speaker, a *Forbes.com* contributing writer, an adjunct professor at the University of Rochester, and the author of business and college planning books.

David has started, sold, franchised, licensed, and taken on partners as well as investors with his companies. He's done it all, and now he is ready to help others start or grow their companies.

David graduated from the University at Buffalo with a Bachelor's Degree in Communications/Advertising. He is also a graduate of the MIT Entrepreneurial Masters Program, an executive education program offered through the Entrepreneurs' Organization (EO).

David's community activities include being a local board member for the Make-A-Wish Foundation, a local board member for Junior Achievement, and starting his local EO Chapter.

In 2004, David published his first book, *101 Things You Can Do To Become an Outstanding Young Adult*. His second book, *Make Love in the Workplace*, a guide to awesome culture in the office, was published in 2014.

David is a prolific speaker—speaking at hundreds of business and education events.

David is most proud of his family in Victor, NY, including three young children, Gianluca, Melania and Alessio. His hobbies include family activities, reading, cooking, eating, exercise, and repeated attempts at humor.

CHAPTER 2

Testing and Lessons

By Mike Bergin

Nobody dreams of a career in test preparation. No matter how many happy, test prep professionals I've spoken with around the world, I've yet to find a single one who planned their path to career satisfaction. As I look back on my nearly three decades of work on SAT & ACT preparation, I can see how I became the founder of the best education company in upstate New York. In my career, I've worked with countless students, families, educators, and counselors on every aspect of test prep and I'm the creator of an arsenal of preparatory resources. I'm also a nationally-recognized expert in my industry and co-host a college admissions industry podcast. But if you had asked me at any point in my progression if this was my plan all along, I'd have laughed.

Almost everyone who teaches test prep falls into the role by accident. Like most of my professional peers, I took up teaching and tutoring mainly because I naturally excelled at testing. As a psychology and social sciences major, I always showed a strong interest in learning and education, but the restrictive nature of conventional teaching never attracted me. However, when an old friend suggested I join him in Boston to start teaching for Kaplan Test Prep—and shared how well the role paid—I had to try it for myself.

A long, snowy New England winter may have dampened my ardor for Boston, but I was hooked on teaching high school and college students to ace exams like the SAT, GRE, and GMAT. So, I returned to my native Bronx and took a part-time teaching role at the Kaplan Center in White Plains, New York. That position grew into a full-time managerial role and, eventually, the director position, overseeing all business activity in seven counties. For the first time, my responsibilities not only entailed teaching, but also all the marketing, sales, operations, and human resources activities required to succeed in the competitive test prep industry. Despite the steep learning curve, I found that I loved the business side of education.

While I loved working with both students and teachers, I often chafed under Kaplan's bureaucracy. Thus, when my former Kaplan boss moved to Huntington Learning Center, I jumped at the chance to help develop Huntington's test prep offerings. He himself didn't last long in his role, so I became the Director of Exam Prep for this national education franchisor, overseeing the department that developed all test prep curriculum, operations, and training. After a round of layoffs, I essentially also became the entire department.

My time at Huntington's corporate office definitely rounded out my professional education. The role took me away from the frontline marketing, sales, and operations I had enjoyed at Kaplan and I missed the student contact I had enjoyed. On the other hand, I mastered the finer points of curriculum and product development, technical writing, publishing, and—once the original No Child Left Behind legislation passed—government grant writing. I also learned a few lessons (often the hard way) about office politics, franchise relations, and organizational accountability.

The curriculum team at Huntington was small and I was the only test prep expert in the corporate office. Thus, I had a satisfying degree of autonomy and the license to create the best curriculum possible within specific, inviolable operational parameters. That is to say, I might not have agreed philosophically or pedagogically with requirements concerning program length and delivery, but I focused on designing SAT and ACT (later SSAT and ISEE) curriculum, training, and support materials that did as much of the educational heavy-lifting as possible. The independence I enjoyed was particularly meaningful for my personal life during this period—I became engaged, married, then became a proud father.

Having children significantly changed my priorities, particularly in terms of where I wanted to raise them. While my childhood in the Riverdale section of the Bronx was a happy one, the combination of metropolitan overcrowding and rampant real estate prices had us looking far afield for a home to replace our tiny, junior-four Bronx apartment. We realized we were in trouble once we started looking at houses a full hour's commute from work. Thinking outside the box—the box being New York City Metro—we recognized that the best move would take us quite far away from the city. Having a job made the move to a completely new area infinitely easier; I approached my manager to explore the idea of dialing down my schedule of three days a week in the office to a more manageable three days a month. Thankfully, through a combination of hard work, responsibility, and results, I'd earned a lot of capital over the years; everyone was on board with the idea. My wife and I didn't waste any time selecting Rochester as our ideal destination, not because of those long, cold winters you always hear about, but because of its proximity to my wife's family. We spent a single Saturday house hunting and moved mere months later in July 2008. I'll always credit this move as the start of a very special period in my personal life, but for my Huntington career, it signaled the beginning of the end.

Upon reflection, the reasons why my Huntington tenure ended so badly still aren't clear. A new CEO came in just as I moved away, so the lack of direct face time might have hurt. The company was also going through a rough financial period with franchise centers closing their doors across the country. It was, after all, the start of the Great Recession. These events put our whole corporate team in a constant state of crisis control. I spent long days remotely, on site, and in the field fighting fires with everyone else, but I wasn't at the corporate office often enough to see the signs up close. Colleagues and I would often joke about how unceremoniously Huntington dumped employees. However, I wasn't laughing when it happened to me. I was laid off right after our Friday morning leadership conference call without notice or severance... just two weeks before the holidays.

While I don't recommend being fired (laid off, excessed, or whatever euphemism you prefer), I found the experience utterly clarifying. As you might expect, my first feeling was panic; I was the sole breadwinner in a household with two young children. The rejection, outrage, and anger would come later, but the first order of business was processing the loss quickly enough to address our long-term security. As we drove to a Christmas party that night, my wife and I sifted through options and struck the course we've followed to this day. She—a licensed social worker—was more than ready to return to professional life. My own options appeared less certain.

My position as product expert and test prep guru at Huntington was an exceedingly rare one, so the prospects of a similar role anywhere in the United States, let alone anywhere in upstate New York, seemed tenuous at best. Moving to other industries would necessitate starting at a lower and significantly less-compensated level. Financial issues aside, I really enjoyed almost every aspect of the test prep field. The educator in me loved the immediacy, relevance, and intellectual stimulation of teaching test prep. My business mind appreciated that in the market, quality test prep commands a premium. There are low barriers to entry, minimal start-up costs, and a predictable path to growth. Finally, the product developer in me who had chafed under design restrictions with which I had disagreed for nearly a decade, started sifting through theoretical models I'd been pondering for years. I thought, "What would my ideal SAT/ACT curriculum look like if I knew it was being delivered by highly qualified, highly trained experts? How much time would such a program require and by how much could the students improve?" Most importantly, "Would Rochester families pay for elite test prep tutoring?"

In a sense, I had no real choice but to explore these ideas. Tempered by fifteen years at every level of the test preparation industry, I possessed all the necessary skills, knowledge, and experience to launch a test prep business from the ground up. After struggling under many ineffective leaders and dysfunctional bureaucracies, I was ready to call my own shots. The entrepreneurial spark that had smoldered since my move from teaching to management began to blaze.

My story becomes cheerfully predictable at this point. Chariot Learning took off. However, it is a mistake to assume that the only things that could ruin a successful enterprise is a capricious boss or a catastrophic event. Sustained success depends on careful, pragmatic planning: what needs doing today, tomorrow, next week, and next month to win in the marketplace? What industry standard processes need adopting and how will we diverge to differentiate our product or service?

My immediate course of action was simple, though hardly easy. While my goal was not full-time tutoring, I needed to take on students while I developed the infrastructure of my professional education company and created the company's new, foundational SAT & ACT prep curriculum. I was relatively new and disconnected in Rochester which put me at a disadvantage, but I started implementing the marketing plans I'd learned and used in my previous tenures. I was gratified to see Chariot Learning acquire its first clients quickly.

Some may wonder where the name Chariot Learning came from, but that's a story for another day. A more relevant inquiry is how I launched Chariot Learning in January 2009, so soon after losing my job at Huntington in December 2008. Technically, we didn't officially launch until much later, but I had already created the Chariot Learning brand years before. My process may prove instructive, even for those who can't see themselves leaving their current jobs for the uncertainty of entrepreneurship. People today often promote the wisdom of the "side hustle," the extra gig, revenue-generating hobby or moonshot project pursued after-hours. The security of my previous corporate job afforded me the freedom to explore alternate business models in the education space. One idea I had that didn't conflict with my day job at the time was around supplemental curriculum. This product would integrate test prep instruction into existing high school lesson plans. The one enduring asset derived from that project was the Chariot name and brand, and it meant a lot when I needed it.

Another critical but unplanned benefit arose from a project inspired by the rise of blogging. While everyone knows about blogging today, I acutely remember when the practice first captured the public's imagination. In fact, I was so taken by the promise of personal publishing that I conceived of an independent test preparation review website powered by a blog. This idea had me so excited that I designed and built a mock site on the clunky Microsoft Frontpage software, only to have Huntington's CEO at the time shoot down the idea. Not only did I learn that in business that asking forgiveness is often preferable to asking permission, I also had a new skillset coupled with a desire to engage in this burgeoning online dialog.

I applied my new skills and passion to another newfound interest—birdwatching—and created *10,000 Birds* (10000birds.com) in 2003. What started as an outlet for my curiosity about the natural world, birding, and travel gradually became much more than that, thanks to my skills as a writer, educator, and marketer. As I connected with more and more people online and in the real world, *10,000 Birds* became increasingly popular. In 2007, Carnegie Mellon declared the site one of the 100 Most Informative Blogs in the world. My side hustle grew to over one million unique visitors a year and has taken me all over the world. Through that experience, I developed potent site building and content marketing skills that really came in handy when the time came to create a website for my nascent educational enterprise!

Creating an effective website with a regularly updated and informative blog was one obvious way to differentiate Chariot Learning from other test prep providers. Another was my plan to treat this business like, well, a business. In this, my training in the business side of test prep separated me from the pack. Most service businesses are founded by technical experts: barbers open barber shops, dentists open dental practices, etc. However, skill as a technician can't completely compensate for inexperience, uncertainty, or incompetence in marketing, sales, and operations. Too many promising services fail to launch because the business owner didn't know how to reach a targeted audience, manage an inquiry funnel or navigate the exigencies of ownership.

Luckily, I knew exactly what to say to potential clients and referral sources. A career in both direct sales and corporate development of marketing and sales scripts provided the ultimate in preparation. Suffice it to say, my initial launch went even better than planned. Even though I had very little in the way of a local network, I quickly realized that Rochester didn't have anyone quite like me offering test prep services, despite a powerful community commitment to education. After adjusting my pricing in response to cues during sales calls, I landed my first client. She promised that if her son's ACT score increased substantially, everyone in town would know about me. Within a month, I was working with her son's best friend as well, and, true to her word, she proved a powerful connector who sent us business for many years... and occasionally still does!

Service businesses like tutoring carry minimal startup costs, so my business was profitable from the beginning. However, when I was the only one delivering services, I didn't really consider it a business. Rather, I had created a good job for myself, one with flexible hours, abundant professional satisfaction, and a boss with whom I finally worked well. The real business began once I'd finalized the first draft of Chariot Learning's curriculum and built a book of business big enough to warrant hiring teachers. Though I'd been working towards that moment from the beginning, staffing promised to be my greatest operational challenge. No matter what anyone else tells you, the efficacy of any instructional relationship depends on two fundamental factors: student motivation and teacher quality. I built Chariot Learning around the concept of connecting the two so success depended on finding and training amazing teachers.

Again, the fact that my business still thrives today gives away the ending but success was never assured. Despite an intense and lengthy training process, my first wave of teacher trainees washed out before they ever met with students. The second wave lasted a bit longer but still failed to meet the standard I knew would set my organization apart. After refining my hiring and development process, I finally struck gold with the third wave of trainees. Three out of four graduated from training and began delivering the Chariot Learning program to high schoolers throughout the greater Rochester area. Eventually, we expanded our physical operations to Syracuse and now have the pleasure of regularly working online with students across the world who hear of our reputation and results. Chariot Learning has, like any enduring enterprise, evolved over its decade-long existence. It has progressed from a primarily one-to-one SAT/ACT business to a business that includes classes, practice testing, subject tutoring, accountability coaching, and more.

Like so many of my colleagues in test prep, I fell accidentally into my dream industry. Like so many others holding on for dear life to their 9-to-5 jobs, I was, through no apparent fault of my own, relieved of that security. What happened after seems like pure serendipity. Everything I'd learned and experienced over the previous decades—all the work and play, triumph and trouble mixed together—prepared me for the most professionally, emotionally, and financially successful work of my life. In this, many more are like me than not. We all have the capacity to turn misfortune into massive success. Don't wait for the crash to learn the right lessons.

What I Have Learned

As I expand professionally into podcasting, writing, business coaching, and licensing, I continue returning to the fundamental lessons I've learned over my long, unplanned career:

1. **Always play with your model and methodology.** We all labor under external and internal constraints at work but only those who understand how to transcend those apparent barriers can truly innovate. At Huntington, my entire instructional framework was based on the number of hours Operations wanted to sell, in conjunction with the quality of teacher the system was expected to produce. Through designing their program within their limitations, I had the perspective to imagine different

scenarios and outcomes from a different set of assumptions. For example, what if I could consistently guarantee superior teachers? Ruminating over that single question for many years meant I had the answer immediately when I finally needed it.

2. **Learn the business of your business.** Too many professionals focus strictly on the technical aspects of their professions. Teachers teach, welders weld and athletic trainers train. That singular focus may satisfy the parts of you that drew you to your profession in the first place but won't be enough to prepare you for business leadership or ownership. Successful enterprises blend the art of technical acumen with the science of business. Expand your horizons and learn marketing, sales and operations in a safe environment before your livelihood depends on those skills.

3. **Challenge your complacency.** While the term "golden handcuffs" dramatically overstates my compensation at Huntington, my situation was rather comfortable, at least, until it wasn't. I appreciated the substantial autonomy of my role so much that I neglected to consider any other. After my completely unexpected layoff, I was lucky that my Plan A worked, because I had no Plan B. Always have a Plan A, B, and C, no matter how much you love your current situation. Just formulating those plans will benefit you professionally and personally.

4. **Create your professional self.** All too often, we imagine that organizations have thorough systems in place to

instantly inculcate employees all of the technical, professional and psychological competencies needed for a given position. Yet, if you just look around your workplace, you know nothing is further from the truth. Take a page from the entrepreneur's handbook and commit to developing yourself for both today's and tomorrow's challenges.

5. **Craft a life you love.** When we talk about work and careers, we often overlook the most important element of the conversation: what we are working for. Many entrepreneurs succeed because of—rather than in spite of— their personal lives. My decision to strike out on my own wasn't entirely based on my vision of a better way to teach test prep. The calculus also weighed numbers such as how much more time I could spend with my children and how many fewer hours I'd waste commuting to a soul-stifling office environment. Anyone who knows me will attest that I know how to take care of myself. Much of that comes from my commitment to creating a business that allows ample time for family, friends, hobbies, and travel. Many entrepreneurs dream of being rich, and, in this, I'm no exception. However, your conception of wealth should encompass all the things that make life worth living.

About the Author
Mike Bergin

Hundreds of thousands of students have aced the SAT & ACT through programs Mike Bergin created, oversaw, or organized... and he isn't nearly finished! A nationally-recognized leader in test prep, Mike founded Chariot Learning in Rochester, New York in 2009 to deliver on the promise of what truly transformative, individualized education can and should be for students in Upstate NY and everywhere else. Mike is also the founder of the free testing and admissions answer site *TestBright*, co-host of *Tests and the Rest*, the college admissions industry podcast, and creator of the Facebook industry group for test prep professionals, Test Prep Tribe.

Mike Bergin is also the founder and co-publisher of *10,000 Birds*, the world's favorite birding blog. Since its inception in 2003, *10,000 Birds* has delivered daily insights into birding, nature, and conservation to millions of readers across the globe. A passionate advocate for the powerful benefits of ecotourism, Mike has been invited to promote birding all over the world.

You can find Mike at http://chariotlearning.com and http://testsandtherest.com

CHAPTER 3

Trusting Your Instincts in Business

By Justin Copie

At 20 years old, with three years of college under my belt, I was ready to light the world on fire. When I started my co-op at Innovative, I went on hundreds of sales calls. The vast majority turned into nothing. But after converting just one customer to buy our services, I fell in love not just with winning but the notion that with the right people, you can change the world.

I became obsessed with learning how to get better. For the next year, I gave up virtually everything in my life—time with those I love, time to find someone to love, and time to have fun—in order to perfect my craft while finishing my degree in IT from Rochester Institute of Technology. Little did I know I would be building a capability that would become the one thing—and maybe only thing—I would master in my short career. I was able to use my words to communicate a message, and influence people's behavior. It felt amazing.

For the next five years, I was on the leadership team of Innovative while working alongside Bob to develop the skills to ultimately take over the organization. I bought Innovative in early 2016 and I really had no intention of changing anything.

From then until the middle of July, every time I walked to the back of the building where a number of engineers sat, the heat would hit me. Clearly, no one had bothered to turn down the thermostat. Seven or eight engineers were seated at their desks, some with headphones on, all intently looking at their computer screens and one was on the phone with a customer. I turned the thermostat down.

There was one engineer whose desk was a disaster; his chair was falling apart and I don't know the last time his oversized coffee mug was washed. It was stained and had a vile saying printed on its side. Once I turned the thermostat down, he looked at me and his face clearly said, "I don't give a fuck."

This was synonymous with how I had let everything "sit" for the past seven months. Once I got to that thermostat, I thought, "If I don't turn the dial—up or down—no one else will." I wasn't asleep at the wheel but we were definitely slowing down and I felt very uncomfortable.

I began to reflect on my journey and professional growth and recalled three distinct times I had thought about leaving the company. For several weeks, I would go home and journal about how I worked myself through each of those times.

Then it hit me—I was able to make a decision once I gave myself permission to leave.

What if I gave my staff permission to interview at other companies? Would they find new purpose? Maybe staffers would find new meaning in their own work, or maybe some would find happiness outside of Innovative. I thought it was an off-chance that an employee would interview elsewhere and find happiness they felt wasn't attainable at Innovative.

In hindsight, I had one goal. I wanted to fill the bus with people who believed what I believed. For whatever reason, we had made it all the way to here and the bus still had those who were misaligned in our company.

This way of thinking was from Jim Collins' *Good to Great: Why Some Companies Make the Leap ... and Others Don't*. It's a book I read nearly a decade prior. I never forgot what Collins said in that book: "A great company understands three things about people—get the right people on the bus, get those people in the right seats and make sure you get the wrong people off the bus." I expect an extremely high level of accountability and I wanted my team to own their place—on or off the bus.

That's how the new mandate "Go interview for a new job" came into existence. On September 23, 2016, I walked into our weekly all-staff meeting and very matter-of-factly asked everyone to go interview for a new job.

I continued, "I think it's important every person in the room seek a new opportunity elsewhere. This is an opportunity for every person to find new meaning. My only request is that you tell us you are looking."

I needed every one of my employees to self-select: up, in, or out. We needed to make sure we had the right people on the bus, and now, this was more important than ever.

Within five minutes of speaking to the entire room, it was obvious I had inflicted confusion, trepidation, fear, and even a little anger onto my team. What did I just do?

Two-thirds of the company took me up on my offer and interviewed for new jobs. Some viewed it as an opportunity to see if the grass was greener, some returned with great ideas for the company and some gained a new-found level of inspiration.

Of course, some left. Twelve to be exact.

Twelve of my friends left the company in twelve consecutive weeks, each handing in their letter of resignation every Friday, immediately following our weekly all-staff meeting. What was most interesting was their definitive feelings to do so. Some didn't even have a new job lined up.

Process that? I sure did. It was emotional hell and extremely draining.

It wasn't until the end of 2017 when things finally felt right. For those who left, they sought a place where they could be fulfilled, and I believe I gave them the autonomy to do that. In hindsight, I wouldn't have done anything different.

By far, the biggest reward from the process was how much we were able to raise the bar when filling the twelve vacant roles. It gave us a chance to recruit an entirely new level of talent. Of those who stayed, there was no question that they were now in it for the long-haul.

Asking people to go interview elsewhere was the birth of what's now called the "Promote Yourself Philosophy." At Innovative, it's impossible to be promoted while in your role. The only way to get a promotion is to self-promote and every employee is required to self-promote within two years. Within that time, employees have to self-select up, in, or out of the company. No exceptions. Even I'm required to self-promote—I play the role of CEO—and it is something in which I take great pride.

As CEO, my self-promotion is an enormously effective philosophy that ensures two things within our organization—immunization against stagnancy and an enormous amount of accountability. My iterations are what I hold as measuring sticks for where I'm heading.

- 2015: It didn't prepare me for running the business. It prepared me to BUY the business.
- 2016: I learned what it meant to run a business.
- 2017: I learned how to effectively run a business.
- 2018: I learned how much I did not know and was comfortable with not knowing.
- 2019: I learned I can trust my gut, and those around me, while running a successful business.

And 2020 will present a new learning. I am constantly going through new iterations of myself and I love it.

Ultimately, there will be a day that I won't be fit to run as CEO anymore. Like Bob and Innovative's other former owners, I'll need to pass the torch by stepping down as CEO and self-promoting into a different role.

I continue asking employees to interview annually. Giving people permission offers autonomy to make their own decisions. Though they may opt for no change at all, it is the construct of our company that enables them to choose a path forward—either with the company or at a different one.

There wasn't a time in these 18 months where I wasn't suffering with a high degree of anxiety. There were a number of supporters in my life who provided me with the strength to get through those difficult days and tough nights.

Bill Knitter, our COO at the time of the buyout, was an incredibly strong supporter of my vision. He, too, was going through a lot of change in his life and we banded together to stay mission-centric in every decision. I owe him my life for that.

Jaime Eisenhauer, VP of People at Innovative, has a brilliant analogy: "If you think of your company culture as a garden, the soil is your work environment, your people are the seeds, water represents development, sun is love and weeds are the negativity that sprouts unintentionally. If you don't give tender love and care to your garden/culture, nothing will grow like you intended."

As we hired those who were aligned with our mission, Jaime fiercely protected the culture we worked so very hard to define. Without question, she was, and still is, a linchpin in our success.

Evan Tzimas, my best friend, was, and is, my go-to for everything needing a sanity check. A major sales contributor for Innovative, he was my guardian angel ensuring I wouldn't drift to a bad place mentally. I love him for that.

Three years later, in 2019, we've grown the business by more than 30%, eliminated major service delivery barriers, eliminated countless single points of failure throughout the business and increased customer satisfaction by a rate of 65%.

Today, our strategy is transformative and our business is recognized as a significant player, not only regionally but nationally. Without asking my team to go interview—by far the hardest decision I've made within my business—I would never be where I am today, with a team that calls Innovative home, with people we consider family.

As I began my journey at Innovative, I learned that with the right people, you can change the world. It is true.

Together, we win.

What I Have Learned

1. **Give your employees autonomy.** Employees that align with our company's vision results in a positive culture and successful bottom line. Our model of giving permission to interview out and internally self-selecting has meant that the people on our bus either get off it for greener pastures, or stay because they really want to be there. Everyone wins.

   Learning is everything. As a CEO I've recognized that every year has brought new lessons. These new learnings can only make every step better and keep myself and our company moving forward.

About the Author
Justin Copie

Justin Copie, CEO of Innovative, is leading the bold move forward: instilling growth in employees and inspiring change beyond Innovative's four walls. The 70 people working at Innovative don't work for him. He works for them.

A respected leader, Justin has built a company culture where it's safe to voice opinions, try new things and, yes, even fail. Justin firmly believes that the boldest breakthroughs and the most brilliant answers come from failing, and so he encourages everyone to learn from their successes (and failures), including himself.

Justin has grown Innovative into one of the top IT firms with the recognition to prove it. Innovative was recently named one of the best companies to work for in New York State by the New York State Society for Human Resource Management and Best Companies Group.

Everything Ends

By Stephen Halasnik

It was 7:00am, September 11th of 2001, and I had just walked into my office. My company's offices are on the 5th floor on a large hill overlooking all of New Jersey. From here, I could see the tops of many New York City skyscrapers about 40 miles away. I had come into the offices with a sense of urgency that day because our monthly revenue had been significantly sliding for the past 18 months. I was worried that what I feared was coming true—the end of a great run might be over and I would have to close the company. From my New Jersey offices, I saw a billowing of smoke on the horizon; on TV, I watched the falling of the World Trade Towers.

I started my company, *EXPERTseeker.com*, in 1996 when I was 32 years old. With grit, determination and hard work, I grew it to over $6 million in yearly sales in four years (an astounding 1,000+

percent). Due to a huge demand for our services, growth and profit was exceptional, but when those towers fell, I knew that the economy would plunge into a recession and with that recession, my company would end. I would have to let people go and I would have to start over. Instead of waiting for our revenue to decline even further, I took action one month later, laying off 95% of the company.

When I was asked to write my story about how I crashed, the first thought that came to mind was that I never crashed. Crashing means that my dreams of owning my own business ended. Crashing means that I failed and never tried again. I never crashed because I always managed my risks and I had a plan before the worst happened. To me, someone who crashes is someone who doesn't survive. I survived and through that survival, I learned how to start again, how to run businesses better and how to reduce future catastrophes.

Over a 25-year span, I have built seven companies with two of them reaching $20 million in yearly revenue. However, each business had huge swings in revenue, profits, and emotions. The nature of all small businesses is experiencing ups and downs. Learning to manage that risk—and emotional roller coaster—is just part of being a business owner.

All business owners who start their own businesses have one thing in common. They are tenacious and total optimists. Building a company is the hardest thing you will ever do so you need these characteristics. If you are lucky enough to build a successful company once, try doing it again. There are so many forces against you, having tenacity is the only thing that will help you succeed again and again.

My entrepreneurship started when I was very young. At an early age, I had a speech impediment and dyslexia. School was really hard for me and back in those days (the '70s), teachers didn't have the tools to help kids like they do now. Not only did I have to work twice as hard as every other student, I had to constantly find a workaround. At the same time, I was lucky enough to have great skill in various sports so whereas schoolwork lowered my confidence, sports built me up. It was obvious to everyone that I was highly motivated, that I always had a plan, and that I was going to outwork everyone until I reached my goals. I was also lucky enough to have parents that knew they just had to get out of my way and I would find my own path. They didn't need to motivate me.

I grew up going to high school and college in the '80s, and the '80s were all about money. *Wall Street* was a famous movie, Bill Gates and Steve Jobs were on every magazine cover. I saw that having money would, first, allow me control over my life, and, second, prove to all those girls and boys in high school that I was special. At the age of 17, I put a plan in place: I would go to work for a big company after college, learn and make my mistakes on their time and then eventually start my own company.

While attending Rutgers University, I went on a summer internship at Xerox Corporation after my junior year. In those days, Xerox was famous. They had a reputation for hiring the best and providing incredible training. I knew that this was an opportunity of a lifetime. I did really well at my internship and Xerox asked me to stay on full-time. Xerox would pay for the rest of my college education if I went to school at night and worked for them in sales during the day. I jumped at the chance, knowing that it was an incredible opportunity.

I worked for Xerox for seven years, becoming one of their top US sales representatives. I loved my work. However, while I worked at Xerox, I continued educating myself about business ownership by reading and taking classes. The more I was promoted at Xerox, the more I saw that my weaknesses in corporate politics were going to really hurt me as I moved into management.

At the age of 29, I was about to get married and my future wife knew about my dream of starting my own company. We decided that it was time for me to start my own business and you would think that after all this time of wanting to do so, I had a great idea about what business to start. I didn't, so I went back to something my mentor said to me. He said, start a business in something you know. So, without Xerox knowing it, I worked ½ a day for Xerox and the other half building my new company— DigiPrint. I did this for 12 months before I decided to dedicate myself to Digiprint.

DigiPrint would take advantage of a new technology called digital printing. Digital printing allowed one to, for the first time, print high quality brochures on demand. This also allowed for one-to-one customization. I worked in this field for Xerox so I knew the industry already. The equipment was going to cost $1 million so what I decided to do was to get the work and outsource it to companies that had purchased the equipment already. This strategy would allow me to build cash flow while learning if there was a market for this technology.

Digiprint made me about $80,000 per year in profit, but after year two, I saw the writing on the wall. No one who owned the equipment was making money in digital printing and the printing industry was so competitive that I didn't want to be in it. I ended up selling my customers for a small amount of money and I was ready to move onto my next business, but again, I didn't know what that next business would be.

I have always read a lot. Reading *The Wall Street Journal* and many other business magazines really helped me understand trends. I knew that large consulting companies like Price Water-house Cooper were making a lot of money helping companies implement enterprise relationship software and other software initiatives. PWC was charging $500 to $1000 per hour for top ex-pert consultants. At the same time, there was a lot written about potential problems with computer code due to the year 2000 changeover. Most computer code was written with the year rep-resented in 2 digits, like YY instead of YYYY. Consultants were getting hired to fix all the code. With all the technology profes-sionals doing enterprise resource planning (ERP) and year 2000 fixes, I knew a shortage of technology talent would happen and I knew that this was a good opportunity for a temporary staffing company.

I also learned from my future mentor that as companies got much bigger, they moved their variable costs (more expensive) to fixed costs, allowing the company to lower their costs and im-prove their margins. Unfortunately, those fixed costs—often full-time salaries and other long-term capital investments—rendered companies unable to respond to market changes. Thus, they were forced out of business or took big losses. I thought the key to long-term survival was not having fixed costs so that I could ride market waves and adjust according.

My sister Denise had started a technology staffing company two years earlier where she brought technology people on H-1B visas from overseas and placed them on assignments. I decided to work with her on a 1099 basis in sales so I could learn the business. After eight months, I believed there was an opportunity to start a temporary staffing company that placed very high-end computer consultants and experts. Many of the best experts were leaving consulting companies like PWC to work for themselves. Whereas these experts used to bill at $500+ per hour and get paid $80 per hour from PWC, I could pay these same consultants $160+ per hour and bill them out at $250+ per hour. These experts were often terrible at getting themselves their next consulting assignments and *EXPERTseeker.com* would bridge the gap. My sister's business placed lower-end consultants and I would place high-end, expert consultants. I knew that I was going to catch a wave. I also felt that while I was in business, new opportunities for additional businesses would present themselves. So, in 1996, I started *EXPERTseeker.com*.

EXPERTseeker.com grew tremendously and the profits were exceptional. So much so that I had to think about reducing my tax burden. I ended up buying a dilapidated 10,000-square-foot office building; it was one of the best moves I ever made. The building cost $150,000 and I put in $600,000 in renovations. I moved my company to the top floor and I rented out the rest. The building is now worth $1,300,000 and generates $80,000 per year in annual net profit/tax savings, greatly adding to my net worth. That passive income and asset has allowed me to leverage the building for a bank line of credit which I used in my businesses.

After buying that building, I realized that I had a real gift—I had a photographic memory with visual images. When we went to renovate the building, like a CAD program I could see every renovation and improvement in my head. I could also picture what might look great in all the spaces and when the renovation was completed, the building was one of the nicest office spaces in the area. People who see the spaces are amazed at the design and decorating.

That same skill set helped me pick our family home. We bought it for $380,000, renovated it so that it is now worth $1,200,000, and it improved my net worth over $400,000 after all the renovations.

The office building and our family home helped me build wealth, leverage financing, and help me survive the ups and downs of future business failures and successes. Building wealth with these assets wasn't exactly an accident. While working for Xerox, I had read a book by Sam Walton called *Made in America* and that book showcased how he lived under his means. That stuck with me and because I didn't buy expensive cars, jewelry, etc., I had assets that helped me when times were tough.

Although *EXPERTseeker.com* was growing, I was still worried because I knew that market changes could affect us. So, I looked at how we could change or add to our businesses. *EX-PERTseeker.com* was first called Atlas Technology Services but about three years into the business, I thought I could move away from our weakness of having recruiters match job openings to using automation for producing the matches (think *Monster.com*). That approach didn't take hold because our customers didn't have the time to search our database. In addition, the experts with whom we were dealing had such complicated expertise that using one or two keywords wasn't adequate for companies searching for a great hire.

I also looked closely at moving to a consulting model, specializing in one area and having full-time employees. However, it was obvious to me that the fixed costs of payroll and managing employees wouldn't allow us to grow over $10 million and I would be tied to full-time employees in an ever-changing marketplace.

I decided to just ride the wave and get as much profit out of the company as I could and when that wave ended, cut expenses quickly to maximize profits, also for as long as I could. That is why when September 11, 2001 happened, I was clear on what I needed to do. In many ways, once I let go of staff, I was kind of relieved. Relieved because I could focus 100% of my time on looking for a better business. One that would grow bigger. One where I didn't have to be the rainmaker getting all the business myself. One that wasn't so dependent on the hard task of finding and keeping employees with exceptional skills. If you are reading this and think that I was a jerk for letting employees go without thinking about them, you have to know that a lot of my employees had a base salary with a majority of their compensation coming from commissions. With our sales going way down, it was best for them to find other work and I often helped them with that.

The key business strategy that has helped me over and over again is having a plan: I have thought through where I am going, how I am going to get there, what obstacles could come up, how to minimize risks and a host of other potential issues. In addition, I don't just think about these things in the beginning of a business but also throughout its life cycle. I always take time out of my week to think.

By the time I closed *EXPERTseeker.com* I had been a business owner for 10 years and I was better at the various aspects of business ownership. From managing people to managing risk to business execution, that experience helped me in future businesses.

EXPERTseeker.com continued to run profitably for another few years after September 11, but I spent the first six months after that day getting myself mentally and physically back in shape. I went to the gym daily, ate right and began looking for my next business by reading everything I could find, making lists about potential future businesses and talking to associates about the next big wave. I had given myself a good runway with the cash I had saved and over and over again, that runway saved me in future businesses. Other than planning, having enough cash or assets to handle tough times is what allowed me to stay self-employed. No matter how good a business you have, tough times will happen.

Many business owners I know ask me if that period was tough. It actually was one of the most exciting times in my business life. I got to start fresh and the burdens of running a business I wasn't excited about were off my shoulders. During that time, I made a list of the 20 or so businesses I could start and I began investigating the most promising ones. In my head, I still had the idea of catching waves but in an industry that was more recession proof.

I started working on an idea for placing temporary registered nurses, doctors, or allied healthcare professionals on long term, temporary assignments at hospitals. Called travel nurses or locum tenens, they would work for 13 weeks and then move on to another assignment in another state. I liked the idea because there was a huge healthcare professional shortage in the United States and I thought healthcare was recession proof. I also felt I had a lot of experience in staffing and that the type of recruiters/salespeople required would be easier to find and train than those required at *EXPERTseeker.com*. I also liked the high barrier of entry required to get into the temporary healthcare staffing business due to the high cost of business insurance.

I started spending a lot of time learning all the phases of this new business idea but I needed an insider's view of the industry. I was lucky enough to speak to a competitor in Tulsa, Oklahoma, who was very kind and informative (throughout my career I have often developed relationships with competitors to share ideas). I asked him if I could fly out and see him. He showed me all the parts of his business: I saw how housing the travelers might prove complicated, that every state had different healthcare professional licensing requirements and that large competitors were locking up hospital contracts. Despite these issues, I felt I had the experience to do well in this business. Looking back, I made one of the biggest mistakes I could, and that has to do with margins. When looking at a business or industry to go into, look at the margins charged and the net profit percentage. If those margins and net profits are big, then it is a good business. However, one of my weaknesses has always been financials and when the competitor showed me his margins, I thought, first, it was good (when it really wasn't) and, second, I felt he was undercharging. I put a lot of effort into understanding the travel nurse industry and when one has invested so much of one's time studying a potential business, objectivity goes out the window. The momentum carries you forward away from skepticism and more towards moving forward.

I decided to start *HEALTHCAREseeker.com* in 2002. We would place travel nurses only and not physicians because the health insurance for physicians cost 10 times what it was for nurses. I felt we could place doctors once we had better cash flow. I felt I would budget $300,000 before I pulled the plug if things were not working out.

With *EXPERTseeker.com*, I started the company in my apartment, just me and my phone. Since the travel nurse industry was growing by leaps and bounds, I didn't want to start slow so I hired three recruiters quickly and a director of public relations. I spent a lot of money on advertising to get nurses. We made very slow progress in growing sales and learning about the industry. After the first year, I had lost $100,000; where *EXPERT seeker.com* had caught a wave going up, *HEALTHCARE seeker.com* caught the wave going down. We got into the industry right at its peak and hospitals started to push back on the expensive cost of travel nurses. Over the next two years, I lost an additional $200,000 and had to let go of all my staff except one really good person. I was at the self-appointed loss of $300,000 and after speaking with my long-time business coach, Jayme, we decided to give it another $50,000 in losses before we called it quits.

Just like the end of *EXPERTseeker.com*, I started looking for my next businesses when I saw *HEALTHCAREseeker.com* wasn't going to make it. That was a scary time because I wasn't sure if I had enough cash reserves to start another business and I might have to get a real job again. Getting a real job was a scary proposition but there was one thing my sister told me that relieved some stress. She said, "You can always get a job and go back to owning your own business again down the road." Like so many times in the past and future, I started looking for businesses in areas which I had a natural gift. One skill I had identified early was real estate development so I started looking at apartment and commercial buildings to buy, renovate and rent. I may not have had enough money but I have never let a lack of money stop me from moving forward.

However, all of a sudden *HEALTHCAREseeker.com* started doing better and it got to the point where I was making good money. Hospitals started hiring travel nurses again and that wave created a demand for our services again. I put the real estate idea on hold and put time back into *HEALTHCARE seeker.com*. We started hiring employees again, but this time, I was much better at knowing what to look for when hiring recruiters and salespeople. Over the next few years, I built a team of really good people and we built excellent processes to make our jobs easier. *HEALTHCAREseeker.com* went from $1 million in yearly sales to $3 million to $5 million to $7 million. We made the 2009 Inc. 500 List of fastest growing private US companies. Not only were we growing incredibly, we had a team of great, talented people with whom I really loved working. Unlike *EXPERTseeker.com*, I was proud of *HEALTHCAREseeker.com*. I was starting to work on really interesting projects and I had a vision that when we reached $10 million in sales, we would look at selling to one of the big companies in our industry.

Through all this, I came up with and started another business called *Credentialagent.com*. This was software that would help hospitals and long-term healthcare companies manage the incredible amount of employee credential information—think licenses, certifications, immunizations, background checks, etc. that expire at different times. *Credentialagent.com* is, to this day, one of my best ideas. It actually solved a unique problem instead of adding a similar business to an already-crowded marketplace.

In 2007, *HEALTHCAREseeker.com* reached $7 million in sales and guess what happened next? The 2008 stock market crashed and the country plunged into the great recession. The great recession was terrible for everyone and every business. Unemployment went to double digits. When people started losing their jobs, they lost their health insurance so they stopped going to hospitals. Nurses who had retired went back to work to make up for their partners losing their jobs. The travel nurse industry was reduced from a $13 billion industry to a $7 billion industry. An incredible drop.

This time, I had a decision to make: would I do what I did with *EXPERTseeker.com* and close *HEATHCAREseeker.com* down or would I ride out the recession? I really liked the healthcare space and I thought we were a really good company so I decided to ride out the recession thinking that when we came out of it, I would have fewer competitors. I knew that a recession is usually 18 months long and I could ride that out, but the Great Recession affected our industry for several years. After three years, I couldn't mentally take it anymore, even though *HEALTHCAREseeker.com* was still making some money; I decided it was time to move on. I gave my remaining staff four months' notice and told them to start looking for other jobs. I closed *HEALTHCAREseeker.com* in 2011.

Over the next few years, I and a close friend of mine, Keith, started looking at angel funding. Angel funding is investing in someone else's new startup. The hardest part of starting a new business is a good idea and we felt that if we looked at hundreds of companies, we would find a good idea in which to invest and provide our advice. A good idea is one where all the questions have answers. Are there too many businesses in that space already? If there isn't any, then why not? What capital requirements are needed? What is the plan and cost to acquire clients? Will you like the business? Do you have the skills to work in the field? How long will it be before you are profitable? What companies might be interested in acquiring your business after it grows?

We got presentations from hundreds of companies and we were just not that impressed with the ideas or the owners. At the same time, we saw how many angel investors were losing money and Keith calculated that you needed to invest in ten startups because nine would fail and the tenth would need to make it big time. It wasn't a formula we liked, nor was it making other investors any money. Plus, we had a hard time finding one company we thought would make it, let alone ten.

Through this experience of looking at angel funding, Keith and I saw that we worked really great together and that we had complementary skills. I was the go-getter and Keith was the one who figured things out. Keith was great at financing/numbers and I was great at marketing. We had known each other for almost 20 years, we both respected and trusted one another as friends and entrepreneurs. I had always been terrified of having a business partner because of the horror stories I heard; this was the first time I met a business partner who made me a better business-person. Keith and I began looking for a business we would start and run ourselves.

Since my Xerox days, I had developed a mentorship with my professor, Will, who taught a class I had taken six years in a row called "Cases from the Harvard Business School." Will taught different case studies about how companies had overcome major problems and he put you in the owner's seat. It was an incredible learning experience taught by a man who not only was a great teacher but he himself was an entrepreneur. I invited Keith to lunch with me and Will so they could meet. Will talked to us about an industry that was really growing—the industry provides short term business loans to businesses that were unbankable. The small businesses to which we would loan money were businesses that Keith and I knew really well because we had built ones like them ourselves. They were staffing companies, machine shops, software companies and many more small businesses that banks just wouldn't or couldn't finance. Also, because clients would pay us back quickly, we would have the ability to use our own money and just keep loaning it back out. Keith was really excited about this business opportunity and because I was so poor with understanding finance, he had to explain it to me. Honestly, I still didn't get it, but I took his word for it that it was a great opportunity. Will had, over the years, told me about the great potential in this industry but because my understanding of numbers was so weak, I didn't think it was ever a good fit for me.

After Keith and I did some more research about short-term financing, we decided to move forward. I called Will to let him know and he surprised me with an angry response. He wasn't happy that we were going into the same business as him. It really shocked me because Will's company had .0000000001 of the market and he had been telling me for years to look into the space. I had a decision to make. Will was a great friend to me but I didn't understand why he was so upset. There was no way we would hurt each other, and in fact, we could even work together. Will was already 75 years old and incredibly wealthy. I even offered to buy Will's company knowing that, for years, Will had been looking for a second-in-command to run the business. Will said "no" to our offer and to partnering; from that day forward, we never talked again. I tried to rekindle our relationship, telling Will that we would not sell to the same clients he went after and we never did.

I decided to move forward and Keith and I started a company called Payroll Financing. Only once in our history have we come across a company that was doing business with Will and we told that company that they should stick with him. To this day, I miss Will's friendship and counsel. He helped me grow in so many ways and his encouragement in good and bad times was critical to my sanity and success.

One of the things both Keith and I often see in a startup, including our own, is the owner learning something that causes him/her to pivot into a new direction or market. I think this is the most important part of a startup. Get into a space with enough cash reserve runway so you can learn and opportunities will present themselves. We started Payroll Financing thinking that we would provide emergency financing when a company was about to miss payroll. We did okay the first two years but the writing on the wall showed us it was very hard and expensive to find clients right when they needed the money.

After thinking about how Payroll Financing could pivot based on what we had learned, I felt what business owners really wanted and needed was a line of credit. I, myself, had one situation with *HEALTHCAREseeker.com* when I was going to miss payroll due to our growth and our bank wouldn't give us a quick answer on increasing our line of credit. From that experience, I strongly believe that every business owner should have a line of credit as a cash backup plan. A source that is easy, fast and inexpensive to put in place. I talked to Keith about it; he locked himself away to study the idea and came back to me a week later with how it would all work. We then changed our name to Financing Solutions (www.FinancingSolutionsNow.com) and started providing lines of credit to businesses and nonprofits throughout the United States. Financing Solutions has done tremendously well and has grown to over $20 million as of 2019. Not only has it done well financially but it has also been the type of business that Keith and I enjoy running, now that we are both close to 60 years old.

The ability for me to start Financing Solutions illustrates an important lesson—one I talked about earlier. If I hadn't saved some money, if I hadn't bought the office building, if I hadn't increased the equity in my home and increased my net worth, I would have never had the ability to finance Financing Solutions. It's why I strongly believe that if you have a business and are not increasing your net worth, then you really just have a job.

In 2014, Keith uncovered another industry in which to start a company with lucrative margins. In 2015, we started Elite Funeral Funding which buys life insurance policies when a loved one passes away, allowing the family access to money for the funeral. We found perfect partners to run the company and we provide financing and business advice. In five years, Elite has achieved $20 million in yearly sales and has run relatively smoothly since day one.

So where am I headed next? Believe it or not, Financing Solutions and Elite Funeral Funding still have issues that require our constant attention. When you are in business, there are so many things which can bring down a company—competition, recessions, changes in trends, new technology. It gets easier but it is never easy.

Every week, I try to find a few hours for studying new, potential businesses but most of my time is spent on what I am good at and what the business needs: lead generation. My job is getting quality prospects for our company and I do this through many different marketing campaigns. I believe that 100% of any company's success is its ability to get prospects coming to the company who then become customers, all at a reasonable marketing cost. The vast majority of my time is thinking of, studying, measuring, and implementing new marketing initiatives. I like my work.

Because lead generation is so important, I decided to accelerate what I thought I would do eventually when I "retire." I am now writing, podcasting, blogging, and speaking about my entrepreneurial experiences. I feel like it can help get the word out about Financing Solutions and it also allows me to express myself by helping other entrepreneurs.

Every day, I am excited to go to work and thankful that I have the ability to still live my dream of owning my own company. Throughout all this time, I just kept my head down. Now, I can look up, reflect, and see how incredible my journey has been so far. I'm extremely excited to see what life has in store for me next.

What I Have Learned

1. **Everything that begins has an end.** Think about what problems could come up in your business and what you can do about them when/if they happen.
2. **Have a plan.** Review and update it often.
3. **Know that the economy has a huge effect on every business.** In an expanding economy, your business isn't as good as you think. A recession will force you to execute your business well to survive.
4. **Every business has opportunities to pivot to a new market, service or product.** Make sure you are aware of those opportunities, regardless of whether you decide to go in a new direction or not.
5. **Building your net worth is key to long-term entrepreneurship and control over your future.** This can come from several avenues, not just one.
6. **Entrepreneurship is autodidactic (self-taught).** You need to keep learning and implementing what you learned.
7. **The longer you stay self-employed, the better you become at it.** The outcome is reducing your risks of failure.
1. **Don't fail, but if you do, pick yourself up, learn from it, and move on.** Resiliency and grit is key.

About the Author
Stephen Halasnik

Stephen Halasnik is currently CoFounder of Financing Solutions (www.financingsolutionsnow.com) which provides lines of credit to US small businesses and nonprofits. Stephen is a serial entrepreneur and over the past 25 years has built seven success-ful businesses in staffing, software, commercial real estate, and financing. A lifelong power learner, he enjoys competitive row-ing and tennis, being outdoors, Buddhism, and being the best dad and husband he can be. He hosts *The Entrepreneur MBA* podcast which helps small companies grow over the $10 million mark.

He can be contacted at steveh@financingsolutionsnow.com.

Preparing For Change: Know Your Employee Benefits

By Shelby George

Precious few are lucky enough to self-identify as an Employee Benefits Subject Matter Expert. It is, indeed, a distinguished title that I just happened to stumble into. I began my legal career as a public defender, fresh out of law school and ready to save the world. I quickly learned that I couldn't hack it. I searched for something else. Anything else. The retirement plan and health insurance industries were the only groups in the private sector willing to adopt a disillusioned "do-gooder" such as myself. Fifteen years later, I'm a showstopper at cocktail parties, regaling strangers with my tales of deductibles and tax codes.

Technical mumbo jumbo aside, the employee benefits industry does scratch my "do-gooder" itch. After all, employee benefits are one of the best, but often overlooked, ways to stretch workers' paychecks further. Tapping into employee benefits is the quickest way to make the most of your take-home pay. Unfortunately, in order to choose their benefits wisely and reap the best rewards, workers must navigate the dreaded and convoluted annual "open enrollment" process. Too often, workers feel forced to select health plans and set contribution rates for benefits that are almost impossible to understand or value, and they get more expensive every year.

I have dedicated my career to making those decisions easier for everyone. I may not be the envy of my friends, but my work is fulfilling. I am changing the world in my own small way.

∝

It was a Wednesday—a day just like any other—when my role unexpectedly changed from all-knowing benefits guidance counselor to benefits consumer. We had received a call from my husband's doctor. A recent MRI revealed a grapefruit-sized tumor on his neck that was so big and so close to his spinal cord that it needed removal immediately. Thankfully, the tumor was benign and the 9-hour surgery was successful. He—and we—are fortunate in so many ways. We survived the system with a broad and deep network of friends and family and I am so grateful. However, despite that good fortune, life is undeniably different than pre-surgery.

My family and I weathered a crisis, but our story is far from unique. Every day, countless others survive much more severe, unexpected events with far worse consequences. According to the Federal Reserve, "during 2017, over one-fifth of adults had major, unexpected medical bills to pay, with a median expense of $1,200. Among those with medical expenses, 37 percent have unpaid debt from those bills."[1] Sadly, this is a problem even for those who have the benefit of health insurance. A Consumer Reports survey of 1,000 insured adults who had a medical expense over $500 in the last two years found that nearly 3 in 10 respondents had an unpaid medical debt sent to a collection agency.[2]

The financial result of a medical crisis can be ugly, but this is only the tip of the iceberg. The financial stress is often only one layer on top of an almost endless number of life-altering challenges. Whether the medical event involves you or someone for whom you care, the doctor's appointments, prescriptions, dietary restrictions, updates for friends and family, and so many other responsibilities can seem unbearable.

During this time, I learned many things about myself and caregiving, medicine and neurology. Most of all, I learned that the employee benefits industry is failing workers. I had a leg up navigating the medical minefield but a law degree and ten years of training in financial services did not prepare me for the emotional riptide of my journey to New Normal. I was suddenly Chief Caregiver, Head-of-the-Household, Family-Financial-Planner, and Grieving-Able-Bodied-Partner-Who-Can-Never-Totally-

---

[1] https://www.federalreserve.gov/publications/2018-economic-well-being-of-us-households-in-2017-dealing-with-unexpected-expenses.htm
[2] https://www.consumerreports.org/credit-scores-reports/what-medical-debt-does-to-your-credit-score

Relate-To-My-Husband. These roles required something new and different. They required an emotional awareness and sensitivity that wasn't part of my on-the-job training. This was a side of employee benefits that the business world did not seem to acknowledge. It had to change.

Five Benefits to Help You Navigate

The upheaval caused by an unexpected medical event is far-reaching and complicated. I don't mean to suggest that it is easily remedied by a private sector industry or a single technology company. However, free or subsidized resources are available, though not often discussed.

Here are five resources to look for:

1.   **Time (preferably paid).** A friend of mine lost her teenage son to cancer. Someone asked her how she was able to get through it. She said, "I don't have a choice. Each morning, I wake up and I'm still breathing." At the time, I found her answer awkward and uncomfortable. Now, it makes sense. When the unexpected hits, the first step is always to get through it. No one can predict how long it will take to get through it or what getting through it will require. The timeline and requirements for one person do not often translate to someone else.

Some employers are more accommodating of this reality than others. It can be tricky finding information about which medical events or family emergencies qualify you for paid time off. Personal matters relating to health are private and I know firsthand how hard it can be to navigate protocols, processes, and legalities around them.

Here are a few places to start:

- If your company has 50 or more employees, check out the Federal Family Medical Leave Act (FMLA). According to the Department of Labor (DOL), the FMLA allows leave for an eligible employee when the employee is needed to care for certain qualifying family members (child, spouse or parent) with a serious health condition. The DOL website defines the key requirements which will help you determine if you're eligible.3

- Check to see if your state has more generous requirements. Currently, California, New York, New Jersey and Rhode Island offer paid family and medical leave, but there are protections in many other states. The National Conference of State Legislatures website offers a chart[4] showing paid time off requirements for each state.

- Ask your human resources manager for an employee handbook and look at your company's time off policies. Asking for a benefits summary or an employee handbook is an effective way of getting a copy of the paid time off or leave policy without sacrificing privacy.

---

[3] https://webapps.dol.gov/elaws/whd/fmla/10b1.aspx

[4] https://www.ncsl.org/research/labor-and-employment/state-family-and-medical-leave-laws.aspx

2. Money for medical bills. Even without unexpected bills, the cost of medical care is staggering. The Kaiser Family Foundation estimates that "a person with employer coverage earning $50,000 annually spends on average $5,250, or roughly 11% of her income, on health care."[5] These numbers are high, yet they are only about half the cost of payments made by those without employer insurance. If you have access to health insurance through an employer, you should certainly take advantage of it. Here are options to help cover medical costs:

- Contributions to a Health Savings Account. Check to see if your employer made a contribution to your Health Savings Account (HSA). If your health insurance plan meets all the requirements, you are eligible to put money aside without paying taxes on it. Some employers make contributions to employee's accounts. If you are not sure, you can ask your human resource manager if your health insurance plan makes you eligible for a Health Savings Account. If so, ask for instructions on checking your HSA balance.

- Call your doctor or health system to get on a payment plan. Usually, a medical bill has a phone number on it so you can call about billing questions. If you are prepared to make at least a partial payment, call and ask if you can get on an interest-free payment plan. If you're prepared

---

[5] https://www.kff.org/health-costs/press-release/interactive-calculator-estimates-both-direct-and-hidden-household-spending/

to pay the entire bill, ask for a lump sum payment discount.

3. **Peace of mind.** After my husband's surgery, I was anxious. My life was filled with constant worry. With some reflection, I discovered that my worry was due, in part, to feeling that my son was completely dependent on me and if anything happened to me, then he would not have anyone left. I was worried about my health, my fitness, my weight, my driving. I was worried about everything because I believed that I had no backstop, no support system. Of course, that wasn't true, but it felt true. Apart from my therapist, the most effective way to manage my anxiety was organizing my Worst-Case Action Plan. The Plan spelled out what financial security I had should the unexpected strike again—an untimely death, disability or a financial shock. When I put pen to paper, I realized that many of the most meaningful pieces of my financial security planning were accessible through my employee benefits:

- Life Insurance. Many employers offer a minimum level of life insurance without requiring a health exam (in insurance jargon, this is called "guaranteed issue"). In addition to not requiring a health exam, it is often much less expensive than purchasing an individual policy. Finally, with some employers, you can elect life insurance for yourself, your spouse or a dependent. Even minimal coverage can help provide some financial cushion at a time when the last thing you want to think about is money.
- Disability Insurance. Similar to life insurance, many employers offer short term disability policies or long-term

policies. These policies are designed to replace some of your income if you are unable to work.

- Prepaid Legal or Estate Planning. Without a will, the state where you reside will determine how your property is distributed upon your death. Despite its importance, only 42% of Americans have estate planning documents like a will or living trust.[6] If you are one of the other roughly 60%, ask your employer if you have access to legal services through an Employee Assistance Plan.

4. Planning for next year. If you are fortunate enough to have health insurance through an employer, you will likely have a one to three-week period once a year where you will have to pick a plan. In insurance-speak, this time period is called "open enrollment." For most people, it is a torturous time of year. Benefits are unnecessarily confusing and often seem written in a strange language that no one speaks. As dreadful as it is, this period is one of the best ways to stretch your paycheck. If your employer offers resources to help you make your open enrollment decisions, it is well worth the time and energy to use them.

5. Opinions on investing. Before Tim's surgery, I had the "young invincible" attitude. I knew that uncertainty existed, but it never happened to me. One phone call changed all that. I no longer felt young and invincible. Instead, I felt like my family and I were the definition of unlucky. Anything bad that could happen, would happen. Both attitudes are irrational, but they drove my spending and saving behaviors.

---

[6] https://www.caring.com/caregivers/estate-planning/wills-survey/2017-survey

After some time, I realized that my financial decisions had become overly conservative. As a "young invincible," I invested my savings in the stock market because I assumed I would never need the money until a much later, future date. Once I was "unlucky," I socked away any savings in cash knowing that it was only a matter of time before I needed it. Neither approach is right or wrong, but especially in the wake of an emotional time, it may be worth getting a second opinion. If your employer offers a retirement plan, ask your human resources manager if there is a financial advisor that meets with employees as part of the plan services. Look at the retirement plan website for educational information. If you don't have access to a retirement plan or you haven't found any helpful information, you can also try your bank. Oftentimes, a bank will provide some helpful resources.

I have always been passionate about employee benefits, but since our experience, I have transformed into a benefits evangelist. I am on a mission to help every worker understand how to tap into their insurance and retirement benefits when they need them the most. Whether you are a "young invincible" or an "unlucky," you deserve to understand and make the most of your benefits package.

What I Have Learned

1. **Health insurance plans may hold more options than you think.** Don't be afraid to ask your HR manager about what your plan has for your circumstances.

2. **Create an Action Plan.** This will help you see what options you can utilize in the event of a health issue and communicate to your loved ones what is available for them.

3. **Look Ahead.** Apart from your benefits, look into savings plans, investments or other financial options.

4. **Find a community.** Whether you are the one dealing with a health crisis or are supporting a loved one going through it, a local or online support group can help you process your circumstances. You might also find new resources and ideas for navigating your situation.

About the Author
Shelby George

Shelby C. George, JD, CEBS, is an ERISA attorney, Certified Financial Education Instructor, Certified Behavioral Finance Advisor, and self-described advocate for retirement savers and health consumers everywhere. She has dedicated nearly 15 years to helping the industry better serve employers and their participants.

With subject matter expertise in the Affordable Care Act, ERISA fiduciary best practices, retirement planning and 401(k) investments, Shelby is a frequent speaker at numerous industry events. In addition, Shelby is frequently quoted for her expertise in retirement and financial planning topics in national industry publications including *U.S. News & World Report*, *Bloomberg Businessweek*, *WealthManagement.com*, and *WSJ Digital*.

In January 2019, she joined benefits technology firm, Perspective Partners, as CEO. Under her leadership, Perspective Partners gives workers personalized, trustworthy guidance that connects them to the employee benefits they need most. In addition, Shelby founded The New Normal Club, a community of support and information for women who are navigating the health shock of a loved one. Shelby is a true financial planning evangelist, on a mission to help Wall Street better meet the needs of Main Street.

CHAPTER 6

Incremental Choices For the Win

By Jason Pero

"This did not go as planned. What did I just do? Is this really going to work?" These were the thoughts running through my monkey mind. It was the summer of 2012 and I had just left my day job. This was my dream since graduating college in 1999—to build up a real estate rental property portfolio that provided me with enough income to replace my day job. I spent nearly every waking moment from 2001 until that point obsessing about investing in real estate. I worked my tail off to the detriment of my health, relationships, and sanity, all in order to work and live life on my own terms. My beautiful wife, Nadia, and I worked long hours at our sales jobs, pooled our savings and worked even more hours buying rental properties in our hometown of Erie,

Pennsylvania. This became my obsession. Money was the obsession. More accurately, the fear of not having enough of it was the obsession. Even though I'd reached my goal with real estate, leaving my day job left me scared shitless and emotionally empty.

What brought me to this point was a mix of arrested development, addiction, insecurity and immaturity on one side, and grit, hard work, determination, wisdom, mentorship, and luck on the other. Growing up like most middle-class kids from a small town, I never really had any teaching in school about personal finances, let alone macroeconomics. I worked a series of jobs through high school and college. Then, I had an internship in college that opened my eyes and exponentially changed the trajectory of my life. I was working for a financial planning company doing the mundane job of going through client files and scheduling appointments for the financial planners. I had been reviewing some files and noticed something that seemed weird to me: One dual-income family was making $700,000 per year with a net worth of a few hundred thousand dollars. This was impressive, for sure, but I wasn't going to be a physician or lawyer like that couple. Then I came across the file of a married couple—a school teacher and a secretary—with a combined income of $70,000-$80,000. This was still a lot of money to me as a college kid making minimum wage. What struck me like a lightning bolt was that the second couple's net worth was $6,000,000. I thought, how is this possible and how do I do this?

One senior planner told me that this couple's secret was not their retirement plans but, rather, that they owned several rental properties. This shaped and shifted my life immediately. I instantly started buying, reading, and immersing myself in every personal finance and real estate investing book I could.

From 2001—when we purchased our first rental property—until 2012 when I left my career as a medical sales representative, I lived, breathed, slept, ate, everything related to real estate investment. My marriage, friendships, health, and career all thrived but ultimately also suffered from my obsession. There's a lot of detail in that 11 years but now close to 20 years later, I can look back and say it was worth it. It was worth it because the lessons I learned led me through a great journey of personal growth, ultimate peace, and satisfaction.

In the spring of 2011, I submitted the letter resigning from my day job. I was leaving after a successful year and thought I could sail off into the sunset. The real estate gig was doing well. But the lure of a steady paycheck and insecurity in my abilities caused me to take back my resignation and instead of resigning, I stayed with the company in a new territory. I kept grinding. A year later, I was put on a performance plan and, ultimately, shown the door. I had mixed emotions. On one hand, here was my chance to fully dive into self-employment, but on the other hand, I was in the midst of closing what amounted to my biggest deal to date. I was also 35 years old and scared to death about failing at entrepreneurship.

At the time, our real estate rental company had several employees and close to 300 rental apartments. Outwardly, I was a success, but inwardly, I was a wreck. I didn't know how to handle my new-found freedom and escalating success. I was insecure. I did not know the management side of building a business: accounting, hiring effectively, managing people, or firing bad employees.

My health started to suffer. Ultimately, I had a near nervous breakdown a few years later. I wouldn't describe that point as "rock bottom," but I did know that I couldn't keep going like I was if I wanted my marriage, health, business and life to thrive. It wasn't as if I woke up one morning and flipped a light switch. From the beginning, I had been constantly obsessed about the areas of my life that I thought didn't measure up. That obsession was the problem. I tried everything I could to improve my life. I started a meditation routine to assist in managing my stress and help me live more in the moment. One thing I realized was that my life was the sum of all of my choices—good, bad, or otherwise. I also realized I was shaped by my mentors, my friendships, the books I read, the words I spoke, and the food I put into my body. You get the picture.

So, now what? Again, it wasn't like flipping a light switch. The saying, "success begets success" has always stuck with me so I knew that all the areas in my life were intertwined. I wanted to get better and improve what was lacking in my life so I could see success overall.

My first thought was, "Holy crap, how do I fix the mess I created?" It would be easy to just coast along. But I knew I wanted more than coasting and that my family, my friends, and my business all deserved a better version of me. I had also become a student of personal development and the late, great Jim Rohn had always said, "Work hard at your job and you can make a living. Work hard on yourself and you can make a fortune." Well, if this is true in business, it must also be true for other areas of life. That said, I had a really hard time putting this philosophy into action because I viewed all the different areas of my life as "all or nothing."

At some point, I noticed that one of my mentors centered his life around a constant pursuit of excellence, as opposed to my practice of "all or nothing." I realized that I didn't have to become a vegan overnight. I could enter gradually—if I ate one vegan meal per day, that was a step in the right direction. I'm still not a vegan, but I generally eat 2-3 vegetarian meals per day. With a better diet (I am still far from perfect), I have more energy for the gym. In regards to fitness, increasing exercise from three days per week to seven is a large task, but going from three days per week to four, then four days to five is easier. Incremental choices.

Becoming a world-class husband and father isn't like flipping a switch either; they aren't "all or nothing" tasks. But spending time with friends who are great husbands and fathers would impact me.

A better diet meant more energy. Having more energy meant improved physical health for the gym. That same positive energy makes me a better presence at home.

But what about those pesky business problems? Seeing a better version of my personal life, I knew I could apply the same principles to my business and they would work. Is it easy to wipe out $250,000 of past-due bills or credit card debt in one go? Of course it isn't. Is it easy to just fire every bad person or element in your life? The answer, of course, is no. More accurately stated, fixing my business problems wasn't easy, but it was easy making positive choices to do so; making the choice to take ownership. Anything good or bad that has happened in my life is a result of the choices made. It is really that simple.

So how did I turn things around? It was my firm belief to strive for continual improvement. I knew then, as I live it now, that life and business either improve or decline based on small daily decisions. Owning my choices and owning the results from those choices is part of that. Eliminate my bad debt or past due accounts in business? Make a choice. My choice was earning more money, paying the debt down first, determining what caused the debt in the first place, and firmly deciding not to repeat my mistakes. Bad employees? Same process. Lack of communication in marriage? Same process.

Turning things from bad to okay, okay to good, and good to great wasn't an overnight process. Even the decision to make that jump was not an overnight one. We are all human. We rise and we fall but we get back up and keep pushing forward.

If you are struggling in any area of life, first know that you are not alone. I encourage you to find a mentor. Find multiple mentors. For me, new mentors, new friendships and new business relationships helped. Podcasts, books, meetups and peer groups are great sources of mentorship. Again, it is all about the small, seemingly inconsequential choices that lead to incremental improvement and lasting success.

An example of this is as follows: I was having breakfast with a friend from the real estate business. He was—and still is—a great friend and always a shoulder on which to lean. He told me that morning about a real estate podcast he enjoyed listening to and thought I would appreciate it. Upon his suggestion, I listened to the podcast and was impressed and impacted. I sent the podcast host an email to let him know that I appreciated his content and that I had learned a lot. A week or two later, the host contacted me back and invited me on as a guest. A year later, I receive a call from him asking me to participate in a beta test of a mastermind group he was looking to put together. This has led to a number of business opportunities, goals set, goals achieved, friendships, business relationships and experiences I never would have had if I hadn't made that one choice to try the podcast.

Don't live a passive life. It will pass you by. Stop thinking about all the challenges you face and all the things that won't improve. Nothing ever happens unless you act. I don't know if you feel fear, insecurity, paralysis or something else. Whatever it is, just remember that one choice—however small or seemingly inconsequential—can change the trajectory of your life into uncharted, amazing territory.

What I Have Learned

1. **All areas of life are intertwined.** Your personal and business life affect each other. Strive for incremental change in your personal life; this will affect your decisions and outlook on your business life and vice versa.

2. **You are not an island.** Find mentors. Listen to podcasts and read books that will inspire and encourage you to make positive changes.

3. **Don't live a passive life.** Make goals. Take the advice and lessons you're learning to make small choices that result in tangible progress towards those goals.

About the Author
Jason Pero

Jason Pero is a full-time real estate investor who got his start in 2001. He purchased his first duplex that year and began building his portfolio while maintaining a day job as a medical sales professional. Jason was able to leave his job in 2012 to devote his time to being a full-time real estate investor. He has owned everything from single family homes to large, multifamily properties exceeding 200 units. He currently specializes in syndications, value-add opportunities, fix and flips, and property management. Jason primarily invests in his hometown of Erie, Philadelphia and surrounding areas, enjoying providing meaningful work and stability to his employees and tenant base. He is a loving husband to Nadia and proud father of Alex and Mia. In his free time, he enjoys spending time with friends, watching sporting events, movies, concerts, and traveling.

Jason can be reached via phone or text at 814-397-8030
jasonpero@yahoo.com
Jason.pero@perorealestate.com
www.perorealestate.com

Workin' to the '80s

By Dr. Kristin Kahle

The entrepreneurial journey is like one '80s song after an-other—some of those songs come with a great dance beat and some are ballads that make you cry. Plus, don't forget the great 1980s hair and shoulder pads! The journey of taking my very young, service-based business and making it into a technology-based company in less than five years has undertones of all the great '80s tunes, including the great hair moments.

In March 2010, President Obama passed sweeping health care reform called the Patient Protection and Affordable Care Act. Like many people interested in health care, I decided to read the bill one weekend. I had spent my career helping employers use their health care dollars wisely; I consulted on what em-ployee benefits to offer, ultimately helping grow other people's companies and put money in their pockets. The first time I read the 3000-page Affordable Care Act, also called "ACA" or "Obamacare"—yes, you read correctly, I read it more than once—I thought to myself, "Employers have no idea what they are in for." Talk about a "Blue Monday"[7] after reading this legislation. Reading about penalties, fines, fees and reporting, ACA would require new technology for sending data to the IRS that many employers couldn't afford. I decided that it was time to help employers with all these new requirements.

All good decisions come in the shower—my service, Navigate-HCR, was created between shampooing and conditioning. It started as a company to help employers and partners with all the reporting, fines and fees under the ACA bill. I was the only one at the time talking about everything that was coming and I think most people thought I was crazy! For my doctoral dissertation, I even decided to write about all the compliance complexities that employers would need to understand under the ACA; it was a fun, 807-page-read, I'm sure! During this time, I was building our pivot tables, Excel spreadsheets and some form of database to understand and analyze the needs of my clients. Then a large franchisee came along and asked for help; that's when I knew this business was a viable one—they paid me a large consulting fee to help them. This was not going to be "Money for Nothing"[8] and I had to deliver something. What that was, I did not know yet.

---

[7] From Power, Corruption & Lies, New Order, 1983
[8] From Brothers in Arms, Dire Straits, 1985

The first year of operations was as a service-based business, looking at how to scale and become viable to sell. Eventually, the decision was made (in the shower of course) that NavigateHCR needed to transition from a service-based business to a technology-based company focusing on the development of our software. My entire career has involved only the use of software, not designing it or project management of software solutions. I had been a salesperson and a national speaker, but my true superpower was taking difficult concepts and making them easy for people to understand. To say that I understood the ACA and could teach others to understand it certainly takes some kind of superpower. As my company was mean and lean, I made the decision to give the software project over to the COO; I was under the impression that she would "Push It"[9] and "push it real good" to the finish line. Her job was getting us a working solution in one year. Reading all kinds of business books about "staying in your swim lane" and within your strengths, I felt confident that my strength was continuing to sell and speak.

I could see that this project was over the COO's head, as well as a challenge for the software company first hired to develop it. Multiple meetings ended in frustration for our staff and myself. The final straw came when the COO left out company 45 days prior to the IRS deadline and we had no viable software with which to work. The company that was hired to develop the software had not delivered a working solution and was holding the existing code hostage. To boot, the product was not even worth

---

[9] From Tramp, Salt-n-Pepa, 1987

a third of what we paid for it. We were "Dancing in the Dark"[10] without code and a viable solution, and time was not on our side.

With multiple clients and partners needing to meet a firm deadline and the IRS certainly not moving theirs, we had to deliver! That meant hiring temps, staying overnight for multiple days, and duct-taping a solution together at the last minute. The '80s song that comes to mind here is "Livin' On A Prayer"[11] or we could even go with "All Night Long (All Night)."[12] Let's just say those 45 days were the worst, longest, and hardest days but we ended up delivering to the IRS on time.

Now the real work needed to begin and that was taking this software—on which we had spent several zeros—and create something from nothing. My background was in health care and business, with several business degrees under my belt. I had to decide what to do and how to run a software company, and fast. Our journey could be aptly named *Starting a Software Company for Dummies*. Let's see: I hired a firm to tell us the code was worthless (I already knew that) and then hired another firm to get us some usable software. The owner of that firm had a meltdown in my office—that was fun—all the while babbling words and phrases that I did not understand. I wrote down all those words, went home and studied them at night. My husband, who is in IT, was extremely helpful with the language and he gave me great advice, "If you want to connect with your developers, you

---

[10] From *Born in the U.S.A*, Bruce Springsteen, 1984
[11] From Slippery When Wet, Bon Jovi, 1986
[12] From *Can't Slow Down*, Lionel Richie, 1983

need to watch Game of Thrones! Get cheeseballs, Mountain Dew and other crappy food in the office kitchen."

"Was that all it took?" I thought. Maybe this was "Welcome to the Jungle"[13] and I just did not know how to survive in the jungle.

Hiring developers and a software firm was expensive and frustrating. The sprint, the scrum, the standups, oh my. What did it all mean? So, I reviewed every book I could to understand the process but what I did not understand is why, at the end of the day, the deliverables of code, products and software were always late! It was time to take control and do things differently. How was I going to change the process and produce a viable software system? There was certainly no rentable software at the time so building it was the only way.

NavigateHCR moved into developing software and creating a way to manage it. We decided to try a new way (for us) to develop software: we took a business approach to the development instead of a purely technical one. We bid out projects, set and tracked start and end dates, created a quickly and effective software testing system and finally, decreased compensation if the project was late. Working in this manner proved effective for us. However, the sales, speaking, and partnership development sides took a hit. Remember my original swim lane? Now I was in a new lane, performing a new stroke. As the owner of the company and ultimate stakeholder, I needed to figure out

---

[13] From *Appetite for Destruction*, Guns N' Roses, 1987

delivery of the software to clients—what fun it is to create software for an area that was previously not automated!

Since I started this with an '80s music metaphor, I will end with a soundtrack and accompanying tips on how to survive and grow your own business "Against All Odds."[14]

The first song is "I'm Your [wo]Man."[15] Ultimately, the buck stops with you. Making decisions is one thing, but running the company's day-to-day and maintaining productivity also needs the right employees and resources.

The second song is "Running To Stand Still."[16] You might think you're moving forward—running a marathon, a sprint, a relay, or, my favorite, hurdles, but most of the time, you're running to stand still. Things will happen around you that you cannot control. The best thing you can learn is how to handle these issues when they happen.

The third song is "Don't Worry Be Happy."[17] As a business owner, you cannot show your emotions to your clients, your staff or your vendors. It is really easy to become frustrated with a situation, but you still have to act happy (to some level). This one is hard for sure!

Then there is, "You Spin Me Round (Like a Record),"[18] Your journey, and the journey that I have experienced, is like a record, one that only those who have lived through it can understand.

---

[14] From *Against All Odds*, Phil Collins, 1984
[15] From *I'm Your Man*, Leonard Cohen, 1988
[16] From *Joshua Tree*, U2, 1987
[17] From *Don't Worry, Be Happy*, Bobby McFerrin, 1988
[18] From *Youthquake*, Dead or Alive, 1985

Spinning around is what happens every day. How you are going to take control of that and take the needle off the record?

The fifth and final song is "I Wanna Dance With Somebody (Who Loves Me)."[19] Celebrate the wins! Know that you have some big wins coming to you and you will need to celebrate. Celebrate even the little wins! Just celebrate! Doing something for your spirit is a requirement on this journey of entrepreneurship.

My final entrepreneurial soundtrack songs come from two very strong women that I love listening to after I get my '80s fill: Meghan Trainor with "Women Up"[20] and Kelly Clarkson with "Stronger (What Doesn't Kill You)."[21] My journey has certainly made me stronger in many ways and I have learned much to impart. My key advice: find a group of people who are on the same journey as yourself; yes, there are plenty of us crazy people out there called entrepreneurs! They will be your tribe, mentors, mentees and your ultimate sounding board. Good luck and I leave you with "Another One Bites The Dust!"[22]

What I Have Learned

My crash and learn lessons are as follows:

1. **Figure out how to get stuff done, regardless of my skills as the company leader and visionary.** By "stuff"

---

[19] From *Whitney*, Whitney Houston, 1987
[20] From *Thank You*, Meghan Trainor, 2016
[21] From *Stronger*, Kelly Clarkson, 2011
[22] From *The Game*, Queen, 1980

I mean how the company operated and functioned, regardless if the tasks were in my swim lane or not.

2. **Get resources, work with resources and ask for resources when needed.** Internally, we didn't have the skills, staff, or time to even try handling the entire project on our own, so we had to learn how to work and partner with suppliers.

3. **Find other business owners on the same path.** I learned that it is lonely running a company; you cannot talk to your employees or senior leadership team. The only person to whom I could talk was the itty-bitty-shitty committee in my head; listening to that one is tough. There is so much self-doubt yet decision-making must move forward. So, get yourself a crew to whom you can talk, a group that understands what you are going through; perhaps they are also on the same journey.

About the Author
Dr. Kristin Kahle

Dr. Kristin Kahle (aka "Dr. K") is the CEO and Founder of NavigateHCR (NHCR), a full-service ACA and compliance technology company. Her team of HR and compliance specialists assist brokers and employers with the most complex requirements of healthcare law. Dr. K, a Certified Healthcare Reform Specialist, represents NHCR in industry-related seminars and summits to ensure her company is current on ACA and other legislative developments, employee benefits trends, and compliance issues faced by employers and HR professionals. Dr. K has significant experience and knowledge of all things compliance and reporting, as she was a benefits broker for over twenty years, previously owned a third-party administrator, and was the first Doctoral candidate to write on ACA/Employer Compliance Complexities. In 2014 and 2015, she was awarded the "Most Influential Woman in Benefits" by Employee Benefit Advisor. More recently, Dr. K was nominated for the San Diego Business Journal Top Tech Award 2019 for the technology developed by NHCR. Passionate about her employer clients, Dr. K started a non-profit, Help for Employers and Employees Under ACA Legislation (HEEL), through which she serves as a lobbyist on Capitol Hill. Dr. K holds a DBA from Argosy University, an MBA from University of Phoenix, and a BA from Pine Manor College. Prior to graduation from Pine Manor College, Dr. K was well-known for being the only female athlete at PMC to obtain a "double-double"!

I Crashed and Seyopa® Saved Me

By Rachel Ellner Lebensohn

My crash was a personal one, not a business one. I had already started my inspirational content and media company, Seyopa®, a couple of years before my world came crashing down around me and I along with it. Like many of us, I compartmentalized my personal life as separate and unrelated to my professional life. As it turns out, however, everything is connected. I also tended to think in terms of my personal life fueling and feeding my professional one. But I've learned that sometimes the work we do can fuel and feed our personal growth and life, too.

We do that sometimes, us humans. We classify, categorize and compartmentalize, and then we rationalize. "This and that" goes in this box, I belong to that box. We forget the common denominators, the connectors and the unifiers that not only render those boxes illusionary but also illuminate how destructive they can be to both our inner well-being and our outer prosperity. We forget that those common denominators are the essence of our humanity: they're what connect us to ourselves, each other and the world around us at the deepest, truest level.

The most common boxes we create are our professional life box versus our personal life box. Yes, there's been great advancement of thought on cultivating and optimizing our work-life balance, but the classification, categorization, and compartmentalization is still present and dominant. The very term "work-life balance" presupposes a distinction and separation of our personal life from our professional one. It says, yes, they're both equally important and we should keep them balanced, but they're separate and distinct.

Since language, nuance and context matter, I prefer the term "work-life integration." Our professional dreams, goals, failures and successes are always integrated (on some level, even if not apparently obvious on the surface) with our personal ones. Why? Because everything and everyone is interconnected. Our experiences, our perspectives and all the wisdom that comes as a result are all intertwined and related. What applies to one box is almost always applicable to another, regardless of how radically separate we may label those boxes. And it goes both ways: our personal lives feed and fuel our professional ones and vice versa. This is a universal truth.

I love universal truths because they're the values, principles, ideas and beliefs that transcend time, circumstances, individuals, and they're always valid. They're the connectors, unifiers, and the common denominators we all share. Often, they're also the simple clichéd sayings we're so sure we already know, or we think we don't need to hear because they serve no practical purpose in the "real" world. In truth though, they're the ideas and concepts that help us navigate our way through the world in the most real and meaningful way; they're also practical, powerful tools in helping us achieve our dreams, both in business and in life.

I used to think that kind of "self-help stuff" wasn't for me. I wasn't judging it *per se*, I just believed I didn't need it. I was a high–achieving, type A, she's-got-it-all-put-together kind of girl. I was an actress-turned-lawyer, a wife and a mom. I had always done well in school and in life. According to the expectations of others, I was "accomplished" and "successful." But that was just it—I lived these roles for the reward of how others would perceive me and I latched onto these roles with vigor, honor, and pride. Today, I also know that I clung to these roles with utter desperation, lest I become unworthy of love if I failed.

In 2009, Bronnie Ware wrote a blog based on what she'd learned over eight years as a live-in caregiver for terminally ill patients. She recounted five recurring themes that haunted almost all of her patients on their death beds and named the blog Regrets of the Dying. When the blog became an internet sensation with more than eight million reads by 2012, Bronnie turned it into a bestselling book called, *The Top Five Regrets of the Dying: A Life Transformed by the Dearly Departing*.

In those final moments of life, clarity and wisdom, all the stuff that doesn't really matter fades into the background and all the stuff that counts comes into focus. According to the book, the most common regret of all was this: "I wish I'd had the courage to live a life true to myself, not the life others expected of me." This regret was shadowed by a deep mourning of all the dreams not honored or fulfilled. As Bronnie insightfully notes, "When people realize that their life is almost over and look back clearly on it, it is easy to see how many dreams have gone unfulfilled. Most people had not honored even a half of their dreams and had to die knowing that it was due to choices they had made, or not made."[23]

We all need reminders sometimes. Even us high achievers and type-As. We can forget what really matters, we can forget our dreams, and sometimes, we can even forget who we are. Our goals slip away from us when that happens, and our world crashes down around us. That's what happened to me.

But everything is a choice, so we can either choose to learn and grow or end up with that same top common regret of those in Bronnie's book. When my world came crashing down, I chose to learn and grow. My intention and hope with my words here, and with the work I do, is to serve as a reminder and guide for you to always choose learning and growth, to always choose to live your truth and not live based on the expectations of others and to always choose the realization of your dreams.

---

[23] https://www.theguardian.com/lifeandstyle/2012/feb/01/top-five-regrets-of-the-dying

"We're on the planet for a relatively short amount of time. Don't waste any of it hiding the truth of who you really are."

– Marie Forleo

We live in a world which dictates that life is about endless hustle-bustle, productivity, and an awful lot of busyness. A world built on the expectations of others, one that glamorizes and glorifies achievement, status, "keeping up with the Joneses," consumerism, and materialism. We are sold a world of information overload, infinite choices, and endless comparisons. Ours is a world in which—whether we're aware of it or not—our definitions of "the good life" and "success" and even our own identities and dreams are deeply influenced and formed by all the above.

It's no coincidence that unhappiness, feeling unfulfilled, disengagement in life and work and a general sense of emptiness is on the rise; indeed, according to Gallup's "2019 Global Emotions Report" as well as several other recent Gallup polls, dissatisfaction with life is at an all-time high! It manifests in a myriad of ways, seeping into both our personal lives and our professional ones: anxiety, stress, burnout, depression, loneliness, addiction and overall lackluster existence. Living with an insidious and gnawing feeling of misalignment, shame, regret and disappointment has somehow become an accepted yet intolerable, soul-eating norm.

For too long, that was me. I had become disconnected and misaligned from my values, my beliefs, my truth, my passion and even my dreams. It didn't look like that on the surface, nor was I aware of it; even if I was aware on some level, I would never have admitted it then. As I've learned and often say, we can't see what we don't want to see. But, once we awaken, we can never un-see what we do see. After my awakening, I could see that I was living a life expected of me, not one that was true to me.

The good news is that we're also in the midst of a climactic turning point and massive cultural shift. Life wellness, spiritualism and personal development principles and philosophies are seeping into both mainstream and corporate culture alike. The self-help domain that was once regarded with stigma has finally disrupted the mainstream and is now cool, sexy, and an essential component of great business savvy and a positive bottom line.

Diversity of ideas, holism, and polymathy are synergistically on the rise, too. We're no longer pigeonholed as much. "Soft skills" like emotional intelligence, compassion, and adaptability are becoming just as important, arguably even more so, than "hard skills" and we're compartmentalizing different ideas and fields less and less. This is all amazing news for us as individuals and for our businesses as we strive to thrive, become our best, maximize our potential, and live our greatest lives! There's less expectation of fitting in boxes and we're more encouraged to uncover our own unique truth, our passions and live accordingly.

"Passion is energy. Feel the power that comes from focusing on what excites you."

– Oprah Winfrey

We can be ambitious and spiritual at the same time. We can possess both creative genius and killer business smarts. We can practice ethicality, morality, integrity, and compassion while still being assertive, decisive and firm badasses. We're able now, more than ever, to integrate passion pursuits and mission-driven, socially-positive cultures and beliefs into our businesses as well as into our everyday lives. There's more encouragement and empowerment to do more of what we love and be more of who we love—all in a holistic and integrated work-life existence and through the multi-faceted roles we play.

I stated earlier that everything is a choice, echoing what Bronnie Ware clearly expresses in her book. She poignantly points out how that top, end-of-life regret of not fulfilling one's dreams is inextricably intertwined with knowing that dreams not honored and fulfilled are due to choices we choose. Sometimes though, our choices choose us. That's how it was for me with Seyopa®. As it turns out, creating and starting my company also ended up saving me. I wasn't aware of it in real-time but, as Steve Jobs said, "you can't connect the dots looking forward; you can only connect them looking backwards."

I see now that Seyopa®, my professional life's true calling, passion, purpose and vision, was borne out of my personal life crash. Somewhere along the way, I had abandoned a huge part of who I was: the actress, film-school attending, creative side of me. But when I conceived of and began building Seyopa®, I discovered a path that integrated all of me—the actress, the lawyer, the deep thinker, the business woman, the storyteller, and even the nurturing mother. In the end, that unified calling also ended up fueling my own personal growth and renaissance in all my different roles and in ways I could never have imagined. It was the amalgamation of all my experiences, perspectives and unique truths that enabled me to create my ideal work-life integration. In turn, it guided me back home to myself, back to living my truth.

I say this to emphasize the idea that we live integrated, interconnected lives despite how rigidly we may seek to separate and compartmentalize the pieces of our life puzzle. It's one puzzle, always. In order to live our best and fullest life, all the pieces need connection and alignment with each other. If your choices and boxes are not aligned with your values, beliefs and truth, and with each other, then you and your dreams will suffer professionally, personally, or both.

My crash was an identity crisis story. I think we all suffer at least one identity crisis in our lives. The details might look different from person to person and our awareness or denial of our crises differ. The people and experiences in our lives either add to our crises or mitigates them. For me, like for many people, and, I think, even more for women in their midlife years, my identity crisis came slowly, gradually, and almost unnoticed.

I started sensing a disconnect with myself. I started losing my passion and eventually realized I was living for others, living a life others expected of me. I felt like a shadow of my former self. Seemingly, I woke up one day and forgot who I was. I felt lost and broken for the first time in my life but blamed and shamed myself for feeling that way. I had become one of those people I never thought I would be—someone who needed some self-help guidance. But again, we all need reminders. All of us.

The path to serious disconnection with oneself is so subtle and insidious, which is what makes it so dangerous. Again, depending on the circumstances and people in our lives, the feeling may remain so subtle that we endure it, ignore it, rationalize it away or blame ourselves for sensing it when it pops up. For some, however, it becomes unbearable and insufferable—we feel like our soul is dying, therefore, like we are physically and literally dying, too. That was me. It gets to a point when we realize that the only way to save ourselves and the people we love is by letting go of the life lived for others. Then we can actually start to thrive.

At this point, I started to realize that Seyopa® had chosen me as much as I chose it, and it was my lifesaver. Making the decision to start my own company with a mission to inspire and empower people to realize their dreams and do what they love served as my own reminder and guide to reconnect my passions, values, beliefs, truth, and power. Creating and building a vision I believed in that was an expression of my truest self reignited my belief in myself, all my goodness and all my capabilities. Those are things we all share and we all tend to forget. As I began to remind others, I too was reminded to love myself again, to honor and fulfill my dreams, and in that process, it brought me back home to myself with a deep sense of understanding. As Buddhist monk, Thích Nhất Hạnh, expresses in his book, *How to Love*, love for oneself first comes from understanding, because to love is to understand. He says: "Understanding is love's other name."

While the initial driver for creating Seyopa® was self-preserving and "selfish" in that regard, as I started coming back home to myself, the journey evolved into giving others that same life-line when they need it. I was in a place to share and express those reminders, those universal truths, those tools that are the guides to "saving people's souls." I could help others reconnect to themselves, to their passions and inner power, to their self-love, and remind them of their deepest selves and their truth. I had the clarity to help others create whatever they felt called to create in their own work-life integration! By doing so, I not only aligned and integrated all the different pieces of my life puzzle, but I also started doing more of what I love and becoming more of who I love. For the first time, I was living my truth.

I'd like to think my crash could have been prevented if I was more connected and aware beforehand of all the things Seyopa® has taught me. The truth is, though, I'm not sure I'd be writing this today or be inspired to create Seyopa® if I hadn't crashed where and when I did. I'm not necessarily saying we need to crash in order to thrive, reclaim ourselves, and create the life and businesses of our dreams. But, to some extent that is what I'm saying because another universal truth is that we grow the most, learn the most and become our most powerful and resilient selves from adversities, from our crashes. If we choose. My mission is simply minimizing the impact and duration of that crash for others and help them make their own choices for learning, growth and becoming their best selves so that they may live their best lives.

We're no longer living in the age of information, we've moved into the age of transformation. Learning and growing from our crashes is a process of true transformation which is rarely, if ever, easy. However, if we can remember to never allow the sacredness of our truth, our values and our core identities become usurped by anyone, anything or any circumstance, then we'll always be ahead of the game. It's easy to say but sometimes the most difficult thing to do. We've been taught to treat others how we'd want to be treated but we haven't been taught to love ourselves the way we love others.

The internal resources are there, we just have to access and reclaim them. I believe that's true for all of us. We all have strength, resiliency and the knowledge of being worthy and loved. We are all here to realize our dreams, live our truth, and become our best selves! So, too, are the external resources available to us—all those personal growth principles and tools are within reach.

There are endless choices and voices in the personal development industry today. Every ideal, theory, idea, philosophy, and notion can aid in the pursuit of happiness, the pursuit of wholeness, the pursuit of fulfillment, and the pursuit of meaning. Of course, there are those—both well intentioned and evil intentioned—who continue to fit these ideals into the old cultural box of material success, surface achievement, etc., all under the guise of answering a higher calling. Thankfully, there is also an army of light warriors gaining strength, numbers, and volume that is making a positive change in how people perceive the world and themselves.

This is the world of personal development, personal growth, self-actualization, enlightenment, and all things good that I am proud to be a part. I am proud to call those light warriors my colleagues, allies, and friends. I am even more proud to see people awakening to the shift—people craving it, yearning for it, listening to the outcry of their souls. I am so proud of those "waking up," the ones I am called to serve, help, and teach. The ones from whom I learn and with whom I grow.

Surrounding yourself with people who inspire and lift you up is an essential component to living your best life. So, too, is reaching out for help, something that can be extremely difficult to do. Understanding yourself, having a growth mindset, taking action, and overcoming adversity all inevitably lead to success. This cyclical, five-point framework: Self-Mindset-Action-Overcome-Success is the foundation upon which Seyopa® rests. Know thyself, cultivate your mindset, take inspired action, overcome any adversity, and achieve success on your terms: your definition of success, based on your truth and based on your self.

"Nothing is impossible; the word itself says 'I'm possible.'"

– Audrey Hepburn

One of the most empowering lessons I learned from my crash is that I can overcome anything! I can create anything! This is not only true for me, but as one of humanity's common denominators, it's true for all of us. Another invaluable lesson and universal truth that helped me so much through my most challenging times is remembering that everything is temporary, both the good and bad.

Personal development champions a myriad of ideas, philosophies, psychologies, and beliefs that can serve as a profound reminder and guide. These "clichés" can help us realize our dreams, live our truth, maximize our potential and live our best and most extraordinary life—both personally and professionally. My dream is for Seyopa® to serve as one of those guides.

The name Seyopa® is actually an acronym made up of the first two letters of its overarching message: Seize Your Passion®. My dream is that the message of Seyopa® allows more of us to live our truth, realize our dreams, and avoid what Ware observed is the number one, life's end regret. My dream is that the messages of Seyopa® will help people reconnect with themselves and their passions, help them do more of what they love, and allow them to be more of who they love. My dream is to inspire and empower people to master and profoundly enjoy the greatest interconnected and integrated game of all—the game of life—both personally and professionally!

Realize your dreams! Live your truth. Become your best self! Be unapologetically you. Love yourself! Because love really is everything and everything really does start with you. Most of all, do more of what you love and be more of who you love. Seize Your Passion!

What I Have Learned

1. **Everything and everyone is connected.** Our professional journey is integrated with our personal ones. One affects the other, always.
2. **Let go of living a life that others expect of you.** Live your passions and dreams now; no end-of-life regrets.
3. **We all have the strength to reclaim our best life.** You can overcome anything and reach the passions and goals you really want for your life.
4. **Surround yourself with those who inspire you.** Today, we live in an age when personal health and holistic well-being is paramount. There is an abundance of external resources, personal growth principles available to you.

About the Author
Rachel Ellner
Lebensohn

Rachel Ellner Lebensohn was born in Tel Aviv, Israel, lived and grew up in New York from ages 5-13, and then returned to Israel for her high school and military service years. She was a professional actress from ages of 5-18, in both the United States and in Israel, working on stage, in film, and on television. Rachel served in the Film Production Unit of the IDF Air Force, and then went on to graduate from NYU's Tisch School of the Arts with a BFA in Film and Television. She also holds a J.D. from the Benjamin N.

Cardozo School of Law and practiced Entertainment Law in New York for several years.

Converging and leveraging her legal experience, entertainment background, and business acumen with her own passions and purpose, Rachel founded Seyopa.com (#SeizeYourPassion!) to help inspire, empower and promote people yearning to realize their dreams, engage their passions, connect with who they were meant to be, become their best self, and attain fulfillment in their lives.

Rachel is passionate, tenacious, disciplined, and extremely driven. She is a dreamer and a doer, committed to excellence and growth, and will stop at nothing to make her vision of living a life full of passion, purpose, and fulfillment accessible and attainable by everyone.

Rachel has two young daughters and currently lives in Delray Beach, Florida.

You can connect with Rachel at www.seyopa.com

From Setback to Come Back

By Karen Calder

I'm a transformational change consultant and mindset coach and facilitator. My life's journey has led me to empowering women and organizations to break free from the confinements of their mental limitations and encourage them to fulfill their highest potential. My secret sauce is my ability to quickly focus in on the heart of the problem and create solutions tailored to the unique needs of an organization and my clients.

Entrepreneurship is something new for me. One could say I am a bit of a late bloomer. After a successful 30-year career with several Fortune 500 companies, I decided to leave it all behind and follow my lifelong dream of owning my own business. The idea of working for someone else no longer appealed to me. I wanted to be in charge of own destiny. I wanted to have greater impact in the world and serve others in more profound ways than I could in a corporate role.

It's been three years now and what a wild ride it's been. With all of the unknowns, failure, and success, I wouldn't give it up for anything. In my practice today, I get to help my clients solve their most pressing problems. Whether it's improving an organization's capability to execute their strategic plans, helping employees adopt (or accept) change, preparing women with high potential for future leadership roles, or support executive women in being authentic while navigating the complex, often male-dominated world of work, I know firsthand how difficult it can all be. It takes a lot of resilience and mental toughness to manage your way through the politics, fears, emotions, and resistance, and emerge victorious, healthy, and thriving on the other side of transformation. Whether it be personally or professionally; it is the same journey for both.

This is me at my best and where I was always meant to be. I enjoy consulting on how to affect change in organizations, and coaching and teaching women how to break free from their self-limiting or sabotaging thoughts. This is my "set back to come back" story and I hope it inspires you to move forward, even if you feel fear.

Q

My father was an entrepreneur. There was something freeing about this that appealed to me as a young girl growing up. I wanted to be one, too. When I was 17 years old, I started my own Power Skating Schools. There was one in my hometown and several in the surrounding townships. My schools were always full. I worked hard often getting up at 5:00am for five days in a row to be on the ice by 6:00am before school started. The profits from my entrepreneurial endeavors paid for two years of university and a third year oversees going to school in France.

Despite my early business success, my father never encouraged any of his children to pursue entrepreneurship. Instead, he drilled it into us that we had to graduate from high school, get a university education, and find a secure corporate role with benefits. Be happy.

Being the dutiful daughter, that is exactly what I did.

During job #3 after my undergrad, I started to notice that something was missing. I didn't know exactly what. I just knew there had to be more to my life than a 9-5 job, then die. I decided to visit my older sister and her family in Florida. The year was 1997. One day during my visit, I went out to enjoy a day at the beach alone. My sister dropped me off at 9:00am and I quickly found a spot looking out over the vast ocean. I laid my towel out on the soft, warm sand and settled myself in for the day. I remember the sun was particularly hot that day. No clouds in the sky. I remember the sound of the waves crashing upon the shore, the smell of salt in the air, and several large ocean liners on the distant horizon. The setting provided a perfect, peaceful setting for me to be alone with my thoughts.

In search of some inspiration, I pulled out my Sony Walkman and chose the cassette tape, "The Seven Spiritual Laws of Success" by Deepak Chopra. I remember listening to it over and over again as these words washed over me, "Everyone has a purpose in life. A unique gift or special talent to give to others. And when we blend this unique talent with service to others, we experience the ecstasy and exultation of our own spirit, which is the ultimate goal of all goals."

"Really", I thought, "everyone has a purpose?" These questions echoed in my head as though on some repeat loop that would never end. "What is my purpose? What are my talents? How can I be of service to others?"

In the stillness of my thoughts, I began to hear a little voice. "Be a motivational speaker, teacher, and coach," it said to me. However, the only motivational speakers I knew at this time were all men, like Tony Robbins. This experience was well before the popularity of Oprah Winfrey and other incredibly gifted women who inspire us today so I kept pushing the voice down. Yet, this voice kept repeating itself over and over again that I could be a pioneer in the field of public speaking, forging a new path. I remember floating in the water feeling excited and alive just thinking about the possibility of being a motivational speaker, teacher, and coach. It felt so right. It felt congruent with who I was. I left the beach that day ready to make a profound change in my life and certain I was going to do it despite my father's wishes.

When I returned to my job in Canada as Manager of Human Resources for a large manufacturing firm, it didn't take long for me to fall back into the life I knew, despite how unhappy it made me feel. I remember telling myself that dream was impossible and that I was crazy for even thinking about it. It definitely wasn't going to pay the bills. It was absurd to think I could be the first female motivational speaker when I didn't have any experience or message to share. Whatever was I thinking?

After a few months, the dream was forgotten, and I moved on to pursue a new job and a new degree. Without even realizing it, I left my dream on the beach. I just wasn't prepared to make the leap of going it on my own. I worked the next 30 years for various companies in a variety of different roles, pushing myself up the corporate ladder.

ℂ

I finally reached my goal; in early 2015 I became an Executive on a leadership team of a Fortune 500 company. I did it! I climbed the ladder and reached the top, I made it. My family and friends applauded me and I wore the VP title as a status symbol of success. But something was missing, I wasn't happy.

The next few years were clouded by perfectionism, people pleasing, and workaholism. I felt like an imposter. I spent a lot of my time trying to convince everyone else (and especially myself) that this was where I belonged and I had worked hard to achieve it. But the harder I tried to "fit in," the more difficult it became. I was working over 80 hours a week, stressed out and disconnected from myself, my family, and friends. My need for collaboration, people first, and inclusion were not valued. The top down approach was just to "get it done." And that meant do more with significantly fewer resources and time. The change brought with it the expectation of working at all hours, under stressful conditions, and no support for myself or my team.

Eventually I hit the "brick wall." I was burnout out, mentally, emotionally, and physically. I couldn't take it anymore. In that moment, I said "no more" and made a different choice. I made a courageous decision to leave a steady pay cheque and successful 30-year career to go out on my own. I had to rebuild my health, confidence, and pursue my passion to work with companies and leaders who value the balance between profits, performance, and people.

Prior to my corporate climb, I always knew I wanted to be a strong voice for female empowerment and organizational change. But I had ignored my inner voice and wisdom for too long. Instead, I pursued corporate jobs allowing a false sense of security to reward me. I knew I would need support. I wasn't equipped mentally and emotionally to go it alone. I needed to find someone to help me connect to my true self and fight the fear of a secure job and the "What if I fail?" mindset.

I found just the coach. My coach helped me transform the negative self-talk and limiting beliefs that had plagued me for years. We worked hard in the mental gym together to rebuild a better relationship with myself. Eventually we unpacked my purpose and built my confidence back up to where it was the day I left the beach.

I've learned that success doesn't come from a pay cheque or title. It comes from being true to yourself, using your talents and gifts, and living your life on purpose. In 2016, I became a consultant, coach and facilitator—paying it forward—and sharing the lessons that enabled me to live authentically with more freedom and joy than I could have ever imagined.

ॡ

Though we are living in the age of self-help books and motivational speakers, it seems that everywhere we go, people are more stressed and unbalanced than ever before. Many are experiencing cycles of frustration and failure instead of living the life of their dreams.

However, there is a secret to overcoming adversity. If you want to experience a life of victory, you must develop resiliency and a strong mental mindset. That means having the stamina to stand through any storm that life brings your way, as well as the tenacity to triumph, even in moments of great turbulence. You must be unshakeable even in moments of uncertainty.

Developing mental toughness is not easy. It is not a quick-fix solution either. It works for those who make the decision to practice it and stick with it for a long period of time. It took me one full year of being in the mental gym every week with my coach wrestling with my thoughts and feelings, learning how to convert them from limiting to empowering. It took me another full year of learning how to master these concepts and put them into consistent practice in my own life. I continue to learn and grow every day as I become more aware of my thoughts, whether they are working for or against me.

While hard work, effort, and persistence are all important, they are not as important as having the underlying belief that you are in control of your own destiny. The key is preparation and starting that preparation now is vital.

I am so glad I bounced back. I learned in that moment that my response to difficulty will determine whether or not I realize my dreams. Never become defined by the insurmountable. Dare to do the impossible! It is never too late.

You will always be challenged. Whether you are in a full-time position or an entrepreneur.

As I write this chapter, I am faced with yet another challenge. I have recently been diagnosed with Stage 3 Uterine Cancer. A very unforeseen obstacle that I now have to overcome, summoning all of my courage and energy while keeping my business running. I know I will overcome this, too. It will be a chapter in the story of my life and will be shared freely to help others find their strength, courage, purpose, and inspire them to live the life of their dreams.

Anything is possible. In this moment of adversity, the silver lining will emerge. It always does. Don't be afraid to step into your truth and the unknown. It's never too late.

What I Have Learned

Here are a few tips to help you cultivate a strong mental mindset and reach for your dreams:

1. **Reverse your self-sabotaging habits and thoughts.** Did you know that we all have a saboteur? We all have our dreams and we all have a part of us that tries to sabotage them, for our "own good." For example, I was working with a client today, who realized that even though she had a good plan, she was never able to work her plan because of the resistance from her self

saboteur. What are your self-sabotaging patterns? How do they show up in your life?

2. **Stop making excuses.** Excuses are the lies we tell ourselves when we're too afraid of the future. Whatever you tell your mind will become a self-fulfilling prophecy. If you don't achieve your dreams, it will be because you made the decision to be imprisoned by your excuses. Excuses will always keep you in a limited place. Overcoming fear is impossible when you're making excuses. You conquer excuses by having the courage to step out and do what seems impossible.

3. **Have faith.** It takes more energy to live a life full of fear than to live one full of faith. Fear convinces you to live within the walls you build yourself. To have faith is convincing yourself to embrace change. You can either live in faith or live in fear; however, faith and fear cannot coexist. When your desire to overcome becomes greater than your fear, it frees you to live authentically. Fear will always attempt to immobilize you, while faith is designed to energize you.

4. **Don't let the fear of failure deter or derail you.** While some would lie down and let their dreams float away, I knew that I had to pursue mine. I felt the greatest urgency to try before it was too late. If I had just given up and resigned my life to a corporate position, I would have never have lived the life of my dreams. Know this. Fear is not real. It is False Evidence Appearing Real (F.E.A.R.). To create success from the inside out, you

have to become aware of your thoughts and change the ones that do not serve you. The way to do this is to notice whenever your mind goes into a fear thought. After noticing, take a deep breath and then put in an empowering thought, like, "I have all I need to succeed." What positive new thoughts do you need to hear? Keep a journal and note how many times a day you are converting your thoughts.

5. **Use your mind and emotions to create your empire.**

   1. How many times do you find yourself focusing on what you don't want? I believe that thoughts become things. Like-energy attracts like-energy and you get what you focus on.

   2. So, what do you usually focus on? The lack of clients, the lack of income, the lack of time? Guess what? That will bring in more of the same. Instead, ask yourself, "So, what do I want?" Listen to what the answer is and stay 100% focused on it.

About the Author
Karen Calder

A former executive at Meridian Credit Union and Walmart Canada, Karen Calder is an influential leader who specializes in leadership development, creating innovative HR/OD strategies and practices, talent management and architecting, and leading complex change projects for Fortune 500 Companies.

As an expert in learning, performance, and change, Karen has successfully worked with companies and individuals in a broad range of fields, including retail, banking and financial services, manufacturing, and consulting.

Karen demonstrates a real passion and dedication to continuous learning and personal growth. She recently acquired her certification in Neuro-linguistics Programming and Effective Intelligence, and is working towards her Executive Coaching accreditation in the field of {Performance and Neuroscience."

Karen holds a Master of Continuous Education, Leadership and Change from the University of Calgary, a Bachelor of Education from the University of Alberta, and a Certificate in Human Resources Management.

CHAPTER 10

Overcoming Betrayal

By Suzanne Doyle-Ingram

In 2009, I owned a marketing firm and was managing to keep afloat, despite the fact that the economy was crashing. We had many of the Fortune 500 companies as clients and we managed their lead generation email campaigns for them, and I naively thought that this run of five- and six-figure contracts would never end.

Until it did.

In response to the recession, some of the companies we were working with froze their marketing budgets and some got bought out by other companies. This meant that our point of contact was now out of the picture and we had to start all over again to win the business with a new person. However, we made it work, and although our revenue was down by about 50%, I felt that we were weathering the storm well and we were still going to be ok.

Then one day, I discovered that my top salesperson had secretly started his own company on the side and suddenly left, taking all our top clients with him! I was in shock. Of course, this happens in business all the time, but I didn't think it would ever happen to me. This man was my friend. I had helped him through so much over the years, including bringing his partner across the country, helping them find a place to live, and even paying for their hotel on the night of their wedding! I really could not understand what was happening because I was so personally hurt. I had never had a betrayal like this and didn't know how to handle it. I started questioning all relationships and wondering who I could trust.

At that time, I was a mother of three young children and my marriage was not good. I felt completely and utterly alone. I had no mentor and no business coach. I was afraid and depressed, but most of all, I felt ashamed. I was ashamed that he had done this to me. I was ashamed that I was so naïve and trusting that I didn't even have a non-compete agreement in place. I could have sued him, but what was the point? The clients had already gone with him and no judge could force them to work with me.

I was also really angry with myself for allowing this to happen in the first place. Many of his clients were initially mine and I had given them to him so that I could focus on running the business. It was actually so simple for him to leave and take them with him.

I still had a few clients left but they were also going through the recession; some had to cancel contracts and many could not pay their invoices. After he left, my income dropped by 90%.

I did not tell any of my friends what I was going through because I was embarrassed. They all thought I had a booming business and a perfect marriage; it was really all a sham. I was too ashamed to tell anyone the truth. On paper, my husband was the "VP of Marketing" but really was not supportive and was always trying new ventures on the side—none of which ever panned out.

I couldn't afford to pay for my kids' extracurricular activities like swimming lessons and dance lessons, so I had to pull them out of everything. I lied and said we were all too busy and wanted to focus on our family. It never occurred to me to ask for help. I don't know if I would have been able to accept help anyway.

I was devastated and felt like a complete failure. I did the only thing that I could do—I stopped everything. I just pulled the plug and took some time to think about what to do next. I have found that when I am stressed and panicked, I don't make good decisions. So, I thought about what I liked to do and what my strengths were. I had always liked writing and I was curious about Amazon's new self-publishing platform so I took a course to learn more about that.

I decided that I would write a book... but I'd write it under a pen name in case it totally failed because I didn't want anyone to know it was me! Actually, I was feeling like such a failure that I was 100% sure it would fail. I used my marketing skills to decide on a trending topic (gluten-free recipes) and worked on the book every night from 10:00pm until midnight when my kids were asleep.

I launched the book a couple of months later, and, to my surprise, it was instantly named a best seller. I accidentally discovered that the big publishing companies knew next to nothing about Internet Marketing and an unknown author could easily sell more books by having a basic understanding of keywords, backlinks, and search engine optimization. The book was selling and I was making money. I then proceeded to write six more books that year and a new career was born.

One day when I was writing on my laptop in a restaurant while my daughter was at a theatre class nearby, an acquaintance approached me and asked what I was doing. I told her that I was writing my 7th book. She was surprised and told me that she had always dreamed of writing a book. She asked me if I would show her how to do it so I said, "Sure!" I went one step further by renting out the local church hall and put on a one-day book writing course. I offered tickets for $99 and sold 20 spots almost immediately. I thought to myself, "If I can do this locally and make $2000 in one day, what if I were to offer it online?" And that is exactly what I did. For 10 years now, I've been teaching business professionals around the world how to write books. I enjoy it so much that it doesn't even feel like work.

I finally came to a point where I was able to realize that if it wasn't for my employee betraying me and ruining my livelihood, I would not be doing what I love today. He actually did me a favor by forcing me to start a whole new career. I had been holding on to the shame and hurt for years and years. It wasn't until I heard Sandra Yancey, CEO of EWomen Network say, "Betrayals don't happen TO you; they happen FOR you," that the lightbulb went off. I am thankful now that it happened, but it took me years to get here.

What I Have Learned

Here's what I learned along the way:

1. **Don't ever be afraid to ask for help.** People will not judge you for it. They want to help you. Be open to receiving help. Sometimes it's hard to be open to receiving it but recognize that and accept it.

2. **Feeling ashamed is not helpful.** When we feel shame, we feel like there is something wrong with us or that we have done something wrong. We feel unworthy and unlovable. I wish that I had been able to overcome that sooner. I beat myself up for years and years. It was a waste of my precious time.

3. **You can retrain your brain.** I was so depressed that my self-talk was very negative. I started listening to guided meditation mp3s every night when I was too stressed to sleep. I also started making a list of all the things I was grateful for. Gratitude works wonders. I would start a new list every day and sometimes it was just: "coffee, fingers that can type, a car that runs, and my back doesn't hurt today". But as time went on, I felt more and more grateful and started noticing all the lovely people and opportunities all around me.

4. **Take responsibility for what happens to you.** Yes, my employee did a terrible thing but I had set up my business to make it easy for him to do that. I had to take responsibility for that. He wasn't trying to hurt me; he was only thinking of himself. How could I learn from this to make sure it doesn't happen again?

5. **Figure out what you love to do and do more of it.** It really can be that simple!

About the Author Suzanne Doyle-Ingram

Suzanne Doyle-Ingram is a bestselling author who has written and cowritten a total of 17 books. She coaches and trains business professionals on how to write and publish books, and how to use those books as leverage to increase their visibility, open doors for speaking engagements, grow their brand and business, and much more.

Over the course of nine years, Suzanne has helped over 700 people become published authors.

She lives in Vancouver, Canada with her three kids.

You can connect with Suzanne at on Facebook at www.Faccebook.com/SuzanneDoyleIngramBiz or visit her website at http://prominencepublishing.com

Do You Have a Crash & Learn Story to Share?

If you have a crash and learn story about overcoming adversity in business, we'd love to hear it! And who knows, maybe we'll invite you to share it in our next book.
For more information, contact David Mammano at david@davidmammano.com.

www.ingramcontent.com/pod-product-compliance
Lightning Source LLC
Chambersburg PA
CBHW062023200326
41519CB00017B/4905